27 VIEWS OF HILLSBOROUGH

27 VIEWS OF HILLSBOROUGH

A Southern Town in Prose & Poetry

Introduction by Michael Malone

eno
publishers

27 *Views of Hillsborough:* A Southern Town in Prose & Poetry
Introduction by Michael Malone
© Eno Publishers, 2010

Eno Publishers
P.O. Box 158
Hillsborough, North Carolina 27278
www.enopublishers.org

ISBN-13: 978-0-9820771-2-2
ISBN-10: 0-9820771-2-2

Library of Congress Control Number: 2009941631
Printed in the United States
10 9 8 7 6 5 4 3 2 1

Cover illustration by Daniel Wallace, Chapel Hill, North Carolina
Design and typesetting by Horse & Buggy Press, Durham, North Carolina
This book is set in a customized version of the Arno typeface.
Distributed to the book trade by John F. Blair Publisher, 800.222.9796

Acknowledgments

ORANGE COUNTY ARTS
COMMISSION

Eno Publishers wishes to acknowledge the generous support of the
Orange County Arts Commission, the Mary Duke Biddle Foundation,
and other donors in helping to fund editorial and production costs of
27 *Views of Hillsborough*.

The publisher also wishes to thank Gita Schonfeld for her invaluable help in
making this book happen and Daniel Wallace for his imaginative interpretation
of the Hillsborough "grid" (and submitting his artwork weeks before his deadline).
Thanks also to Speed Hallman and Gail Cooley for their careful reading.

Many, many thanks to our twenty-seven authors, a choir of Hillsborough voices.
These writers are not just gifted, but have been remarkably generous with their time
and their work. They also were punctual (or at least had unassailable reasons for
delay). A special thanks to Michael Malone and Allan Gurganus for their efforts,
counsel, and unflagging enthusiasm.

Permissions

Some of the works in this volume have appeared in whole or in part in other publications.

The poem, "who will be the messenger of this land," by Jaki Shelton Green, copyright 2003, Carolina Wren Press, Inc., appears courtesy of Carolina Wren Press.

"Reborn Again," by Josh Kastrinsky, is based on an article originally published in the May 27, 2009, edition of *The News of Orange County* and appears here courtesy of *The News of Orange County.*

Katharine Whalen's "Stop Your Engines" is based on a story originally published in *The News of Orange County* and appears here courtesy of *The News of Orange County.*

A version of the Introduction was published in *The Chapel Hill News* in 2006 as "Falling in Love With Hillsborough," by Michael Malone.

A version of "Going Up the Country," by John Valentine, appeared in the *Independent Weekly,* www.indyweek.com.

A portion of Allan Gurganus's essay, "Old Houses & Young Men," originally appeared in the Spring 2000 *Alliance for Historic Hillsborough Newsletter.*

A version of Jill McCorkle's "Dog Hunting" originally appeared in *The Oxford American.*

A version of Hal Crowther's "Cedars of Lebanon," was first published in *The Oxford American,* and is the concluding essay in *Cathedrals of Kudzu* (published in 2000 by LSU Press).

A version of Holly Reid's essay, "The Ice House at Burnside," appeared in the Fall 2002 issue of the *Hillsborough Historical Society Journal.*

Lee Smith's *On Agate Hill* © 2007. Reprinted by permission of Algonquin Books of Chapel Hill. All rights reserved.

Michael Malone's "Uncle Tatlock and the Town Clock" is based on an earlier version of that story, published in 2003 by Tryon Publishing.

Table of Contents

Preface   15

Introduction by Michael Malone   17

❧ A PLACE CALLED HOME

Allan Gurganus   23
   Old Houses & Young Men: *Notes on Renovation & Survival*

David Payne   49
   To the Eno: *An excerpt from* Barefoot to Avalon—A Memoir

Beverly A. Scarlett   53
   Views of the Eno

Peter H. Wood   65
   Settling In

❧ STREET SCENES

Bob Burtman   73
   Identity Crisis

Thomas J. Campanella   81
   Hillsborough in Time & Space: *A View From Afar*

Elon G. Eidenier   91
   "Dinner at the Saratoga Grill"

Josh Kastrinsky   93
    Reborn Again

Mike Troy   97
    "Always"

Aaron Vandemark   99
    Edible Hillsborough

 VIEWS IN FICTION

Randall Kenan   109
    Hillsborough: Where the Wild Things Are — *a very short story*

Michael Malone   115
    Uncle Tatlock & the Town Clock

Lee Smith   125
    Scenes from *On Agate Hill*

IN THE COUNTRY

Hal Crowther   141
    The Cedars of Lebanon

Elon G. Eidenier   147
    "You Can Walk the Eno"

Nancy Goodwin   149
    A Gardener's Journal

Jill McCorkle 155
 Dog Hunting

Craig Nova 159
 Deer Drives

John Valentine 167
 Going Up the Country

Katharine Whalen 171
 Stop Your Engines

❦ VIEWS FROM BEFORE

Jeffery Beam 177
 "For We Were Once a Wayside Inn"

Brooks Graebner 181
 A Temple of Justice Amidst Temples of the Lord:
 A View of Courthouse & Churches in Hillsborough

Jaki Shelton Green 185
 "who will be the messenger of this land"

Barry Jacobs 189
 The Journey to Hillsborough

Tom Magnuson 195
 The Name Game

Max Preston 201
 "Hillsborough Speaks (*Prologue*)"

Holly Reid 203
 The Ice House at Burnside

Preface

YEARS AGO, a writer friend from western North Carolina had just published a book and wanted to read at the Hillsborough Literary Society, which novelist Michael Malone and I had resurrected. The society hosts about a half-dozen literary readings at the Burwell School each year, emphasizing but not limited to local writers.

We'd love to have you read, I told him, but we've already scheduled the entire season with Hillsborough authors. Lee Smith had a new novel, as did David Payne and Michael Malone. Jerry Eidenier had a new collection of poems. Historian Peter Wood had published a book about Winslow Homer.

I urged him to check back next year. He did. Hillsborough writers again filled the calendar, with a line-up that went something like this: Hal Crowther, Jaki Shelton Green, Allan Gurganus, Nancy Goodwin. The following year: Jill McCorkle, Randall Kenan, Craig Nova, and other local authors.

I guess I'll have to move to Hillsborough, joked my friend.

The busy calendar of author readings is just one of the signs that the town has become a literary locus. Per capita, Hillsborough outpublishes any town in the South, and probably in the U.S. Well, I can't back that up statistically. But check out the ever-expanding Local Authors section at one of our local bookstores (yes, we have *great* ones in our area) and many writers whose works are featured on those shelves call this tiny hamlet home. Or peruse the fiction and nonfiction sections of bookstores around the country and you'll find that many of our hometown writers enjoy national reputations.

Writers have brought much to Hillsborough. And Hillsborough contributes much to them. Be they poets, essayists, novelists, journalists, historians, memoirists, writers eventually write about home. Sometimes the town is front and center. Sometimes it provides a backdrop. Sometimes the town is celebrated. Sometimes the frayed seams of its complicated past and complicated present are examined.

To have a town documented in so many genres by so many skillful practitioners from so many perspectives is a rare phenomenon. *27 Views of Hillsborough* offers twenty-seven of those perspectives. It is a book about a sense of place.

Welcome to Hillsborough.

— *Elizabeth Woodman*

Hillsborough, North Carolina
January 2010

Introduction

IN CASABLANCA, "Everybody comes to Rick's." In Hillsborough, everybody comes to Churton Street, where sidewalks bustle with shoppers carrying parcels and waiters serving outdoor diners under market umbrellas. Everybody comes, and more and more, they fall in love.

A few years ago, the National Trust for Historic Preservation named Hillsborough to its list of America's Dozen Distinctive Destinations, an annual ranking of unique and lovingly preserved communities. "Hillsborough is a perfect Southern host—charming, hospitable, and always fun," said Trust president Richard Moe. "While Hillsborough cherishes its history, this is no staid museum exhibit but a vibrant town with an eye firmly focused on the future."

Hillsborough certainly has a past. Its downtown blocks commemorate so many crucial scenes in our nation's founding that drivers do not have time to read the historical markers, even slowed by traffic as they go through town. It had a past in 1000 AD when Occaneechi Indians lived and traded here. It had a past in 1771 when Revolutionary firebrands fought the Royal Governor at the Battle of Alamance, years before Paul Revere galloped into Concord, Massachusetts, and yelled that the British were coming.

Hillsborough was already a flourishing Colonial hub when the North Carolina delegation met here to demand that the Continental Congress in Philadelphia add a Bill of Rights to the Constitution. In the antebellum South, the town was famous as an educational center for young women and men both, and it was from Hillsborough's Dickson House that General Johnston surrendered the largest army of the Confederacy to General Sherman.

But as the Alliance for Historic Hillsborough proclaims, when listing the town's sights and sites, "It's not JUST about history." The truth is, all kinds of people love Hillsborough who don't know Mrs. MacDowell Hogg from Hog Day or Thomas Day (the freeman furniture designer whose exquisite nineteenth-century pieces are coveted by museums) from Thomas Ruffin (first chief justice of the state supreme court, who in the one-room law office that still stands in our front yard wrote two seminal American legal opinions—one articulating the principles of eminent domain and the other, *State v. Mann,* codifying the legal ramifications of slavery). For Hillsborough has the capacity to keep re-inventing its major enterprise—farms, academies, mills, law, and government—while holding onto some quintessential quality that makes people want to be here.

It may be apocryphal that in the 1930s Hillsborough turned down the chance to host the Rockefeller Colonial reconstruction that instead became Williamsburg, Virginia. What's undeniably true is that Hillsborough takes pride in its genuineness. "Who wants to be a reconstruction? We're real."

In vibrant contrast to the strip malls and suburban complexes that stretch indiscriminately from state to state, there's a particularity to Hillsborough, a human scale to its brick storefronts and frame eighteenth- and nineteenth-century houses that feels authentic, local, as alive as good literature. You wouldn't be surprised to see Tom Sawyer whitewashing the Colonial Inn (which could use it) or Scout Finch and her father Atticus shopping for a watering can at Dual Supply, a hardware store that looks as it did fifty years ago—the way a hardware store ought to look.

These literary analogies are pertinent. Hillsborough is chock-a-block with writers, perhaps more novelists, poets, essayists, scholars, and historians per square foot than any other small town since, well, Concord, Massachusetts. Within shouting distance ("Free for lunch?" or "Randall Kenan's reading tonight," or "Let's put on *A Christmas Carol!*") may gather on any day such talents as Hal Crowther, Nancy Goodwin, Allan Gurganus, Craig Nova, David Payne, Jill McCorkle, Lee Smith. And that's just a few blocks of the list.

More than two dozen writers have contributed their fiction and verse, their research and reflections, to 27 *Views of Hillsborough: A Southern Town in Prose & Poetry.* This would be quite a collection if the participants were limited to Americans only or North Carolinians only. That this gifted group all lives in one small Piedmont town, and that dozens of other local writers will appear in 27 *Views, Volume 2,* makes this book even more remarkable.

These views are from all sorts of directions, just as people come to Hillsborough for all sorts of reasons. To shop, to eat, to hear blues; to see Montrose Gardens; to study the Revolutionary War; to stroll through that (now sadly rare) phenomenon, a walkable downtown. They go to the historic Burwell School where Elizabeth Keckley once lived as a slave. After buying herself out of slavery, Keckley went on to become dressmaker to Mary Todd Lincoln—and so the pre-eminent couturier of Civil War-era Washington society. They visit the Old Cemetery where a signer of the Declaration of Independence is buried. People who visit the town, come back, more and more often, to look for a shop, a book, a project, a house, a dream. Someday perhaps they will come to a community arts center to see a play.

There are sometimes arguments between those who would preserve the past and those who would clear it away for the future. But from its picture-perfect old courthouse to its sleek new galleries, Hillsborough looks to embrace a past and a future both. Brooks Graebner, rector of an historic, local Episcopal church and a passionate advocate for historic preservation, for modern diversity, for the arts, and for Hillsborough, imagined that future when he said that Hillsborough is destined to make an "ever larger contribution to the cultural resources of the area, the state, the region, and the nation." The citizens of Hillsborough believe in that destiny, just as did the citizens in 1871, in 1771, and in 1471 before the first Europeans arrived.

Sooner or later, everybody comes to Hillsborough. We already knew that we were a "Distinctive Destination." It's not just about the history. But we've got that too.

— *Michael Malone*

Hillsborough, North Carolina

A Place Called Home

Old Houses & Young Men

Notes on Renovation & Survival

ALLAN GURGANUS

History and whimsy make people move. Wars relocate millions monthly. Epidemic drove me from Manhattan. But where should a nomad go? After all, you have to live somewhere.

In 1979, I'd arrived in the great city. Just past thirty—I was frisky, driven. I found a cheap apartment and invaluable friends my age. Also writers and painters, they'd escaped little burgs in Iowa or Georgia. Hometowns had told us all: We walked too fast, lived too hard, expected over-much.

Being outlaw-aliens, we christened one coffeehouse ours. There we praised and criticized each other's art and hair. Within six month, we'd become the skinny overeducated kids that old-guard New Yorkers wanted decorating their parties. —If you're visibly young, relatively pretty, and even secretly talented, what cannot be yours?

We published our first cutting-edge stories, showed our early paintings. And—for two years—felt that Manhattan had been built for us as Disneyland is Mickey's.

The disease proved ambitious as we, if far more effective. Within months, it trapped us. To get into a hospital, to qualify for some third-floor bed, you must—at the desk downstairs—present a card. We did not have that card.

Those youngsters just called "most gifted" were being daily felled by a flu from horror films. We now met—not at chi-chi East Side parties—but in fluorescent charity wards. Sick friends were tended by their young friends spared as yet. Sitting bedside, we watched Manhattan's brightest handsomest kids lose forty pounds of muscle in six weeks.

Church-going parents from the Midwest and South, informed by phone of their children's fate, resisted visiting or sending checks. "You had to go and pick New York City, didn't you? Well, you got yourself into the mess. . . ."

Later, parents in black confessed regrets. "Never thought we'd 'lose' him. We saw this as a little life-lesson. We were only trying to toughen him up."

From a cemetery in the borough of Queens, I could see New York City shining. Distance shrunk its silver spires to wedding-cake-centerpiece-size. Metro real estate is valuable even out among the dead of Queens.

Here, gravestones stood packed shoulder-to-shoulder: subway rush hour driven further underground. Manhattan was just more markers, a boneyard annex. Warning: When the city you most love starts looking carved of cemetery marble, it's time you relocate.

In nine years of partying and artistry, our crowd had sacrificed thirty amazing people under age forty. I'd somehow survived. I'd written a book, published it, even made some money. That seemed improbable as everything else.

After certain funerals, you can feel so exhausted you fall back to some spiritual default setting. Your soul? Room temperature. Time to hit "Reboot—All Systems." If anything can save you it might be your body's blind animal faith. Your built-in magnetic North. (Or South.)

We left the graveyard. We were chauffeured back into Manhattan. Tonight's stretch-hearse seemed the celebrity limo we had all secretly expected on arriving. Approached from a cemetery, the skyline looked sulfuric. No longer a pop-up-invitation, our city was a giant sympathy card.

But, however dazed I felt in that backseat, I did recall one rustic fact: I had been born in small-town North Carolina. Even nomads started somewhere. Might that not be my logical next spot, last stop? The soil of my home state is red-clay. Surely its base-coat comprised far more of me than the city's recent silver-plating. Were "going South," "buying the farm" only defeatist terms? If I skipped town after just eleven years here, wouldn't my dead friends consider me a quitter? Can you trade an expired community for another you don't yet know exists?

After the jaggedness of New York, everywhere else would be blunt, dull. But, having just buried the last person I imagined I could save, I felt finally off-duty.

I saw myself pursuing some big old house in a small village in the state I knew best. 'Dull'? That was all I could handle after the complexities of history, epidemic. Tonight I felt fugitive. I felt like the last Jew to recognize he must flee Nazi-Berlin. The hearse-limo slid to a halt before my building; the doorman, respectful, removed his cap. I ran upstairs and started packing.

"Plan B" for Southerners is always: Return.

My West Side apartment contained a house's worth of vintage clothes, eighteenth-century furniture found on the street, life-sized plaster saints, art works by those newly dead. I would need one huge truck to do my litter honor.

What made me so fervently believe that tender Shelter elsewhere might shield me, might help collect myself? I pictured, as through haze, one old house waiting. I knew this place would fit me—tailored, personal as armor. I had a shaping goal now. Find it.

What, in my own grandparental heritage, made me always feel safer-saner inside the castle-keep of some old house? The best of such places were those owned by my family or me. I hail from the merchant class, persons militantly land-poor. Go hungry if need be, but never rent, only own.

Window-glass belonging to you, it's always the best corrective lens.

Sit indoors, stare outdoors, reconsider.

2.

Our parents taught us: You don't know a town till you've seen "the old part." Driving our state, we would veer off highways to explore. As kids we soon learned that, like the structure of all flowers, towns have classical numbers of very similar parts.

Early in our lives, my brothers and I could tell a Colonial house from a Victorian one. We were likewise schooled in the names of every bird, most trees. This was considered less a liberal education, more some manly course in common sense.

Our folks believed even vacations should educate. (Mom had the faith of a poet, the strength of a spinster Presbyterian missionary sent to China. And, alas, that Master's in Elementary Ed.) As kids on holiday, we mostly longed, not for Constitutional History, but theme parks and waterslides. Still, Mother made her four whining sons tour battlefields, lighthouses, houses, the birth hovels of most U.S. Presidents. Maybe my willingness to risk New York had sprung from her own geographic moxie.

During holiday car-games we played aloud, Mom asked what kind of shelter we would choose if offered any house we liked. Would we design one ourselves, or might we take some old one that same size? Even her youngest, then about five, picked an ancient homeplace over any structure merely new.

(There are many ways of dividing humankind and this, I guess, is one.)

Our vacation expeditions veered toward cotton gins and manor houses, through countless crumbling beautiful nineteenth-century downtowns. What mattered, what soon shone for us was: visible evidence of the history of a thing. It seemed to hold some power of attraction peculiar to a Source.

Such automatic reverence can, of course, lead you to powdered-wig pieties, right-wing thinking. All middlebrow lovers of history court sententiousness. And it's here our poor Dad comes in.

While touring Williamsburg, he had pointed out one ancient fir tree. Propped on crutches, it'd been kept alive by every arborist's trick short of IV drip. "Boys, just think . . . Why, if that tree could talk. . . ."

Smart kids are Rhetoric's bitter little enemies. We soon punished Father's having an imagination merely Republican. His four wise-ass sons, crowding his claustrophobic station wagon, were soon announcing, "If this penny could talk . . . it'd probably say . . . `I wish I was a nickel.' If that cow could more than moo, it'd probably go. . . ." Etc. ad nauseam.

Our father, driving, suffered a reddening of both ears. This usually indicated incoming apoplexy or an extrovert outburst, both. He, unlike that tree, *could* talk. Scream. Dad stopped the car. He threatened to leave us all beside this a-historical road in alien Virginia. "History is no excuse for sass."

You want to bet, Dad?

3.

My parents were relieved I left New York. Mother cried on the phone. She'd come to consider the city itself infectious. The folks blamed that sudden terrible disease not on my wayward sexual and artistic life but on Metropolis itself.

They'd come to know my friends, to like then love them. During the parents' Broadway and shopping visits, my pals cranked up their considerable charm. Pals joined us at restaurants only my father's credit card made possible. And now, with that circle expired or scattered, Dad and Mom welcomed me back to home turf reclaimed.

I hid my apartment treasures in a North Carolina storage unit. First I camped out in Chapel Hill. I preferred my own company. It contained last traces of my missing friends' in-jokes, big talents. I secretly considered myself the unofficial Widow to thirty pals of both, of all, sexes.

Some months along, I put myself in the hands of a very pretty expert who sold historical properties. I had earned enough from my one book to make at least a serious down payment on something old. She drove me to beautiful Federal homes, one wonderfully called "Pilgrims' Rest," then to a horse farm called "Maple Hill." These fine homes were already on the National Historic Register. No paint color could be changed without written permission from a panel of gentlefolk. I soon saw these homes as safe, arranged marriages. They came with historical dowries and guarantees. But some essential mystery, the profound pant-level attraction, felt missing.

I lived on in a cottage of eight hundred square feet. I tried nursing myself back to—not health—but at least toward feeling like someone opaque. There is a kind of tiredness that makes you sense you're see-through as a ghost. Times it seemed I was sleeping like a bat, in some cave, upside down, a hanging icicle, brittle, six feet long, dripping into nothing.

—One afternoon some local friends, scouting for land to buy, invited me to ride along. Beloved local acquaintances seemed bent on keeping me at least in motion.

We turned off the major highway and into an eighteenth-century burg. It looked as sound asleep as Rip Van Winkle just before his alarm went off. The town's very stillness spoke to me. Such silence was certainly not urban. But if you listened, you heard tucked within it: blue jays and mocking-birds and, was that a church organ? Yes this was Sunday morning. Families bound for worship, crisply dressed, walked hand-in-hand toward music then steeple bells. Our car passed the Old Town Cemetery circa 1750. One immense magnolia, with buttress-tendrils like a banyan tree's, shaded half-an-acre's sculpted graves.

And right beside this boneyard, hidden behind briars and one gigantic holly, I saw an enchanting two-storied house. Of Arts and Crafts vintage, it was sort of a cottage but something like a mansion, though with some candy-box stab at picturesqueness. Its concept of "Home Sweet Home" had held up pretty well since, what? 1900. The place appeared beautifully built if lately not maintained atall. (A cedar tree had grown five feet tall in its second-story gutter!) Out front, no "For Sale" sign, alas. But the home's noble decrepitude, familiar from my recent New York medical life, seemed another cry for help.

"Whoever gets that place," I told friends, "will be the luckiest person on earth."

Six weeks later, dear reader, that house was mine.

There's such a thing as love at first sight.

I live in it.

4.

My mother and father survived long enough to visit this site of so much necessary renovation. I rejoice that they saw me here settling in. My quiet folks understood how unlikely had been my own survival. They savored finding me joined, as in cohabitation (if not yet legal marriage), to this drafty belfry they admired. The place gave us all a belated sort of peace.

I wanted my parents to be my first houseguests. I imagined finally giving a grand party not a memorial service. I wanted to make my house seem a good home to my folks. And, of course, the house was a consciously forged refuge where certain young New York friends might hang out. My rooms were filled with trophies of them, their paintings of me and each other, their early books. Here they might've relaxed from the big careers they all so rightfully expected.

I have now lived in this house for sixteen years. I came South hoping to hide till dying. And, for the longest time, I managed such hiding. Dying, being an acquired taste, keeps its own schedule.

I'd found a town so small that, on weekends, its quiet seemed a meadow's. For a while I managed to survive far back indoors. I hid even from my own inviting front porch. I stole only out into the hidden rear-garden. But, the very act of renovating any old place, it has a way of renewing, while unnerving, he who writes the checks.

Odd, by now, the house so reminds me of my grandparents' place I can't recall *not* owning it. But possession itself can be dangerous, blinding. Your own childhood's force-fed Colonial history can make you seem just another history-minded fuddy-duddy. Decades keep passing at whistle-stop speed; and your neighbors might never guess that you, of the white beard and the bedroom slippers, once lived as a handsome hotshot artist when Manhattan was still innocent of epidemic. Locals could think you've had nothing better to do with your time and earnings than just to gussy up another village house. I came here to hide. But, at best, I live here only half-eclipsed.

My new-old burg—the 1750s state capital—is now populated by a skeleton-crew of five thousand souls. Three thousand remain mercilessly Baptist. Nine hundred are mildly Presbyterian or gently Episcopalian. The rest of us live undeclared. But all of us, no matter how we chanced to wash up here, have become unwitting snobs about our streets' Federal architecture.

Whatever grip History still has on me, whatever lessons my conscientious parents managed to pass along, whichever diplomatic skills I've hatched in getting out of many kinds of trouble, these motley knacks have all been employed reviving one Edwardian bungalow. A lost cause—my favorite kind.

5.

"On the cusp between 1880s gingerbread ornamentation and 1900s Arts and Crafts blond and ebonized woodwork, this lumbering Victorian can boast an unaccountable attempt at Moorish (?) flair." So a half-informed realtor's listing over-boasted.

The house had gone unpainted forty-five years. Its Gothic porch showed would-be Alhambra arches. Its wood had long ago got wind-burned the silver of some old Jefferson nickel. The one deacon's chair left on its big porch lacked even a single straw of its woven seat. A true (now bottomless) deacon's chair.

Widowed, one old woman had owned and loved the place. Living alone, clerking in a local drugstore, she could not afford its upkeep. Instead, using her stubby broom more stick than straw, the widow spent Saturdays sweeping its sidewalks (then, needlessly, its whole crabgrass yard). By madly circling the decaying manse, enacting a cleaning ritual, she at least publicly proved her good intentions, her former membership in a fickle club called The Middle Class.

She pinned her long white hair on top. Given her affection for that broom, neighbor-kids soon called her place "The Witch's House." Kids lacked the nerve to venture up its cracked walkway onto its sagging porch even at Halloween. They rightly knew the broad front hall must smell of moss, mothball, and old persons' habits.

A society of squirrels had long since occupied this structure's very walls. My first night, I was not alone. First I heard scratchings that were either the ancient builders of the house warning me away, or else my recent dead trying to establish residence on the third floor prior to revealing themselves to me on the second or first.

Come midnight I realized it was only a civilization of squirrels. A chaos of them. Rodents' attic-relays thudded over my bed, sounding like a kindergarten's three-legged race.

Squirrels considered the home's old-timey fabric-wrapped wiring one long and salty pretzel of rare delicacy. A single light bulb still worked. And yet, at first sight, I'd fallen for this crippled dive. Reassuring that houses' life-spans can run to centuries. I knew I was joining an already long list of those who'd loved this place.

It seemed partly Brothers Grimm while also Andy Hardy upbeat. It most recalled the spirit of my grandparents' place. That house still stands an hour and a half away (if now painted by strangers an awful industrial blue). You don't purchase an old house. You marry into it. And I, as the hyper-responsible and probably tedious eldest of four kids, have always been ravaged by rescue-fantasies. My love life has suffered accordingly! This place at once called out, "Please, try and hold me up? Then I'll help hold you, forever. Amen."

I'd bought the place from grown children of its lady-owner. They promised to leave the premises "broom-clean." Instead they flew the addled old gal off to some Arizona retirement home overnight. They'd abandoned an unwanted fridge full of food rotted absolutely lacy; potato salad showed the gray-yellow-greens most often seen in Science Fiction. I waded, upstairs and down, through enough saved paper bags, enough expired soup coupons, enough shoe-trees and hairbrushes and empty 1940s Kleenex boxes to literally fill twelve dump-trucks. Such un-citizenly behavior by the children of the former proprietor at least absolved me of ever needing to communicate with these deadbeats ever again.

I was left to feel still more heroically the rescuer of a once-handsome home very nearly run to ground. In 1900, some unnamed local contractor lovingly shaped this place of heart-pine, a russet wood so resinous it has a tensile density of steel. "Heart-pine" is a homeowner's valentine of a term. I soon recalled that description of Sir Lancelot, "He has the strength of ten because his heart is pure."

6.

During the seventeenth century, a craze for secret societies helped spread Masonism. Part of its mystic symbology involved faith in preferred geographic sectors; these were demarcated by so-called "ley lines." Such marked zones offered benignity, propitiousness, purest energizing luck. And, three city blocks from me, an Anglican church was built on such a grid's preordained goodness. I swear my house enjoys this potent geological mo-jo, cosmic traction.

I credit that with bringing me an honest contractor—bearded, gifted, funny. He is still a friend. The soil surrounding my house somehow proved fertile for my old roses and the lilies growing gigantic atop six-foot stems.

A revered cemetery next door provides outrigger silence. From my thirty-foot desk, carved as open angel wings by a brilliant local craftsman, I look out on certain calcium deposits called gravestones. —Ranks of upright obelisks celebrate one signer of the Declaration, one unsuccessful candidate for U.S. Vice President. The encircling stone wall shepherds many a kneeling marble lamb. Graves' wide spacing proves: Coffins here get far more growing space than those in boneyards with views of Manhattan.

The Colonial cemetery offers my fictive inventions an implicit test-audience. Graves become our ship's crew, lending their names to my invented characters. They give sponsorship to my infrequent garden parties and to the daily labor here at this keyboard. As I type, I literally oversee the illustrious dead (without, I hope, ever overlooking them).

7.

Manhattan had magnetized us. First settlers called it "New Amsterdam" before the later English revised that to "New York." It seemed a novel place to begin afresh, to be young and wild and talented.

In this village I'd sought something else. A spot for the repetitions of the middle years, the deepenings of the latterly ones. Not antiquity so much as custom. I'd moved here to be alone with thoughts, artifacts, memories, and the clean starts offered by ten thousand blank pages.

Now, after nearly two decades here, certain local rituals have taken on the consolations of liturgical repetition. Friends and I stage open-house

Halloween tableaux-vivants at this address. Our fête at the former "Witch's House" is open to all neighborhood kids and any adult willing to find a mask.

I treasure another annual performance, a two-person of *A Christmas Carol*. It is performed, at a Gothic church of the correct Dickensian period, with my friend, the novelist, Michael Malone. I play Scrooge. Typecasting. The town calendar forms itself around a hundred other voluntary rites and homemade entertainments.

This place once teetered at the edge of squirrely ruin. By now, it feels nearly comfortable as such gabled places from my not unlucky North Carolina boyhood.

34

Some nights, turning out the porch light, I swear I occupy my grand-parents' headquarters. (Its still-magical-sounding address was 712 Marigold Street.) Their house, like mine, enjoyed the over-elaborate foreword of a restful front porch.

I have new respect for the pains my grandfolks took with home maintenance. When I was sixteen, I sneered at fuss over roof tiles and chimney-cleanings. My grandmother had once famously remarked, "I'm in bed at seven o'clock from pure exhaustion. I've had four men working in the yard all day!"

At last, I understand. Forgive my having ever smirked at you, my "Big Momma" of the perfect red tulips, the geometric hedges.

I once found it deranged, my family's concern for a certain brand of lemon floor wax. It had to smell one citric, zesty way when any person first stepped into our front hall. (A single place in Pennsylvania still made it; my grandparents swore they'd bought out the whole last job-lot. I'm still using it today.)

My contractor and his helpers left after one year and a half spent camped here hammering. Then I noted my staff was considerably smaller than my late grandfolks'. Fact is, the staff is mostly me. Plus anyone I can afford to hire now and then by the hour to help me clean and paint and patch. A trustworthy high school boy cuts the yard only when need be. What a luxury to have that automatically occur. Oh, the wasted hours of my adolescence!

Like so many kids of guys who won World War II, I grew up irritably Suburban. Our barn-red rancher had more windows than an advent calendar. Its lawn proved as bland as high-maintenance, a losing combo. Bare hardwood floors always felt punishingly cold beneath a child's feet. Nothing architectural seemed much older than I.

In my childhood ranch house, there was one dark corridor leading from my parents' bedroom to their bath. It felt the very marrow of Home. The floor was over-patterned with piled-up orientals; its walls were literally paved floor-to-ceiling with photos, drawings, daguerreotypes, of us. Of family. Family in history. I could mull and browse here. Sometimes I'd drag the clothes-hamper from their bathroom. Then I could crawl up high enough to see some like-me great-uncle on the back row in a team-shot.

They say talent skips a generation. Maybe that's true architecturally. Our chic efficient ranch home, monopolizing two acres on Fairview Road, could not compare with the earlier wonder of my merchant grandfolks' would-be mansion. Near the old-town center, ancient oak trees lined their street. Gigantic roots buckled sidewalks. Neighbors, on foot, came calling every Sunday.

Sabbaths my father, his five local siblings, and their large broods convened here after eleven o'clock service. The communal sit-down meal for forty remained, with Church and School, one unassailable weekly feature of our lives. The big house made such crowd-scenes feel intimate. It proved bathrooms enough and sufficient hiding-places kids require. The garage out back had, not that long ago, been a stable. Old harnesses and tack mildewed turquoise-blue still hung from rusty nails beside a new black Packard gleaming its implied horsepower. Nothing ever got thrown out. Because you never knew.

My grandparents presided. Their vertical house framed them to advantage. Tufted parlor furniture seemed proud of its maroon velvet. Grandmother's "French" wallpaper showed redundant leisured shepherds. Our Sundays' heavy midday meals here made each of us feel, briefly, rich.

Upstairs, a warren of bedrooms had been abandoned by our marrying aunts and uncles. Sports trophies and girls' vanity tables had been outgrown in the 1930–40s ancient-times. Leather football helmets and cheerleaders' pleated skirts still stuffed closets. Here, behind closed doors, in familial darkness, beneath the tickling encouragement of dress hems and tweed sleeves, certain kissing, certain sexy petting-experiments found cousins offering themselves to first cousins. First come first served. Keep it in the family. Practice, practice, before ever involving judgmental strangers with alien eye-and-hair-color.

Kids, bored on rainy days, were denied usual visits to a schoolyard's swing-sets just across the street. We instead retreated to the second floor, re-dressing in our parents' old clothes. We'd make thumping entrances downstairs to general approval and applause. Somebody would always say, "I can't believe I ever fit into **that**!" This person's spouse got a big laugh by too readily agreeing.

And now I have a house. Its walls are hung with photos of my dead young friends; its book shelves feature first and second novels by kids manic with starter promise. Some porch rockers serve as secret portraits of expired pals. These make my house a family home, if for one particular kind of family. "Some men propagate, others decorate," so goes an easy joke. And it seems plain that love of Home-life is sometimes most zealously celebrated by those denied full marital-and-legal rights to it.

This old home — seen by strangers from the street — what sort of family must it seem to house? Does the off-brand-answer make mine less a family?

I am sometimes asked, "You live alone in all these rooms?" Yes and no.

I was once grilled by a local husband and wife, "Why would someone like *you* need a station wagon?" (Does a bachelor's furniture, mulch, and friends weigh less than that of the normative married?)

How do you answer that? And should a property-owning taxpayer really have to?

Is this domicile—containing one bachelor, his very old ancestors, and his very young ghosts—really earning its keep?

Don't ask, don't tell.

8.

Even in a town just five thousand strong, even if you try and hide, your house hardly stands alone. Village lore soon enriches you despite yourself. Go register to vote and see if the widow poll-watchers will let you leave without a chat, without news of one candidate's sudden third marriage and how much his old home is going for two blocks over.

You walk back to your own place. It is the one you chose to believe in by becoming, for so long as ye both shall stand, its present-occupant-spouse. Sure, you're just her latest swain and suitor. And, at tax time, or come the hour of mandatory re-roofing, you'll complain of being her shamelessly exploited Sugar Daddy. But the rewards, if private, can finally feel conjugal, profound. And you get this bonus: A house cannot silently rise at 3 AM and pack and *leave* you. Fires excepting, it should survive you.

Of course, I subscribe to the village paper. And, last week, one of those local Southern women who lives to be 110 was again asked the secret of her great age. (Newspapers never tire of presenting one group of people with the same question over and over, do they?)

"How *have* you stayed alive so long?"

"Keeping inner-rested."

"And," the reporter at least showed enough enterprise to add, "what, over your century and ten years has interested you most?"

The answer came, slow, as if laden with compound interest.

The birthday girl said, "Dark chocolate and red wine. Old houses and young men."

9.

My home was built during the last century's infancy: the golden age of The Barbershop Quartet and, for that matter, The Barbershop. While pruning and cleaning this manse, while beating its acre of hardscrabble ground into some form of garden, I'm still finding poignant evidence of earlier intelligent life.

Though I might appear to live alone here, I do not. Who needs ghosts in a world so brilliantly material? Domestic archeology, the proof of others' plundering land-claims, can make a house feel (not less yours) but far *more*. Since 1900, many souls have, like me and mine, considered this barn all theirs:

I found charred evidence of a small fire started then quickly doused in the farthest corner of my attic. (Some candle-lit shrine? Someone hiding up there overnight and beginning to feel cold?)

I found a basement noose suspended from the crossbeam at child-height as if for the creepy execution of stray cats.

I found six WW I toy soldiers made of cast lead, and two rubber khaki-colored WW II ones rendered gorier by lavish daubings of very red fingernail lacquer (filched from Mom or Sis?).

I found a huge diamond engagement ring that, upon more careful examination, proved merely a "diamond-like." At first glance, I imagined that this jewel would help me pay for a renovation that cost, as always, double what I could even vaguely imagine someday eventually affording. (At times, I marvel that I am not in jail!)

I found that a friend who'd considered buying the place years before had chanced upon a leaf fire in its backyard. From ashes, she rescued, still intact, an eighteenth-century ginger jar. She made a gift of it to me when I moved in: gray and white Canton ware, hand-glazed to depict arched bridges, long-haired willow trees, and four huge scissor-tailed flying birds.

I found, wedged beneath one loose hearth brick, a much-creased yellowed love letter from a married person addressing another married person wed to still a third. Judging by the dates, and their immense implied kindling-pile of crushed longing (secret meetings at a farm outside tiny Mebane, NC!), they are now long dead; but at least one lover wanted this memento discovered; and I discovered it. No names, please.

I found a revivable garden volunteering strange hellebores; I found a rare white hyacinth favored in the eighteenth century and escaped from the graveyard next door. I found many of those lilies called "pink naked ladies," flowers that shoot up leafless overnight then go off all at once like private fireworks or some gold-and-rouge fifteen-year-old beauty flashing you. I found how well a butternut banister responds to lemon oil. I learned that this 3200-square-feet family house, built wide-across-the-beam before the days of effective contraception, still loves absorbing hordes of trick-or-treaters. Still eager to accommodate crowds, it can hold ninety people without, as we say of pregnant women, "showing."

10.

Till recently I did not believe in ghosts.

About certain persistently falling picture frames, about the mystery of midnight lamps that snap alight unaided, I will not complain. (That would be unseemly. Like grousing about your adored longtime mate in front of harsh strangers you've just met.) Certain mysteries are part of any complex, and therefore successful, cohabitation.

A decent house at least one century old will not allow you to merely live IN it; you agree to live WITH it. It secretes quiet currents that direct you without your really even noticing. Why, for instance, is your main room never quite used, whereas the pantry's suddenly everybody's favorite hangout? What so determining once happened in each place? What matron of which race ruled where?

You soon live amid emerging traces of all previous owners. These are not just bookmarked by that single heavy Bakelite deco earring; they register via certain half-map spirit-rivulets of moods and daydreams not quite yours.

Old houses spill their hidden facts in miser's coin or sudden terrifying jackpot.

One of my best friends spent over thirty years in a home nearby. Hers was built circa 1906. Here she and her husband brought up their three children. Here, that same husband, reaching the itchy age of fifty-five, bounded home one day to announce that the sight of his wife's visible wear-and-tear made him feel suddenly old, whereas his secretary, twenty-one, reversed such achy tasteless hints at his mortality. So he was out of here. "But first let's divvy up the kids' baby pictures."

My friend, having said good riddance to "her first husband," remained loyal for another two decades to their original homeplace. But approaching eighty, she herself was now about to leave. Losing a fair share of her eyesight, she would say goodbye to a house suddenly too large, one story too many, springing all sorts of sudden costly leaks, on a street turned abruptly "bad." So be it. She had had her time here. She'd created the garden by which most gardens in driving distance were now measured. She'd rendered a stolid home more beautiful and welcoming, far sounder, more lovingly mythic for her forty years spent in it.

And only now, as she stacked favorite art books into ugly detergent boxes, only after all these decades enjoying the place as its hostess, docent, mother, only now as she decamped, did certain other presences—happy here earlier—fulfill a long-intended need to make themselves known to her.

Since my friend's eyes were faltering, since ghosts are said to be as notoriously see-through as certain successful shower curtains or négligées, these former occupants contrived to bless her exit by offering themselves as signal smells.

I'll let **her** tell you:

"The first arrived as pipe tobacco. I mean, that old-fashioned apple honey shag nobody uses now. For three days, I would be sitting in various rooms, packing things. The smell would start up in puffs, little comings and goings, always just behind me. As if someone had settled right in back of me to watch or encourage my book-sorting, to somewhat keep me company. Next day, a young friend came over to help me organize the last of our library. We both sat here quietly working when I smelled the country-sausage. It was cooking just two rooms off. Homemade sausage, full of sage and herbs and smelling somehow French and really wonderful. (The kind of sausage you can only still get around here sometimes out at the Red and White in Dortches.) Finally I turned to the young girl helping, and asked while trying to sound offhand, 'Smell anything?'

"'You mean anything besides the sausage? That our lunch? So kind. Who's in there cooking for us?'"

There are certain mysteries. To know them, undertake a current-interest-rate mortgage on something old to ancient. If such places were able to talk, they'd fail to remain mysteries. So, Sphinx-like, they instead keep their own council. "If that tree could talk . . . it probably certainly wouldn't."

Instead, the spirit residues of your home's former citizens—they perfume you, tease you. They offer hints of presences both scarcely there and yet far more permanently present than either you or I.

They, after all, have come through that cruel if incidental audition we call Death. (Whereas you and I have not. Not yet.)

11.

Since the village street plan here is an eighteenth-century grid of chummy lanes and deep-set chimneyed houses, walking to neighbors' homes remains a pleasure for modern legs and eyes. I mean: Distances and vistas are great enough to entice but not exhaust you. I'd rather hand-deliver notes to friends' front-porch mail-baskets than bother with a postal stamp or e-message. You feel the ancient scale in such a simple starter-unit of community. Not unusual here to find some anonymously offered plant or pie-slice left on your porch. My *New York Times* gets tossed onto the sidewalk from someone's moving car at 5 AM.

Between that hour and my getting out the front door an hour and half later, some kind stranger often carries my paper the thirty feet clear up the walk and onto my porch. There it rests. Who does this? I could wait out there and try and catch my helper. But, I prefer not knowing. It might be young ghosts or old ones in powdered periwigs. It might be some beautiful living jogger. It could be anybody.

42

I moved here as a retreat from a world too real. I wanted to do my work, to keep to myself. But the world—like those junior high games that force boys from one side of a gym-dance to partner those girls wall-flowered opposite—the reel of village life won't take "no" for an answer.

My creating a hermitage for this hermit seems a failure. I was too quickly caught up and, sometimes chafed, taken in by some enriching weave of ancient legend and present hunches. I am a chess-pawn set on this board of gravestones, gubernatorial obelisks. I live amid tired jokes, ancient trees, and certain vertical houses that've proven persistent as our nation's life. I mean, of course, I am trapped happily here in history's daily making and forgetting.

It is a setting predicted by all those boyhood car-vacations to see farmhouses where generals breathed their last. Historic markers call our village-homes by the names of their builders. Such persons were often dead long before our great grandfolks ever saw light. Likewise, the gossip in a settlement so old and small as this never stays merely contemporary for very long. "Meet Miss Smith, new here, and who has already done so much to shore up the Rouhlac-Nash house, `Pilgrims' Rest,' where Ogden Nash's grandparents spent the first War and where the three-year-old heir-ess to the Pettiford millions fell down the spiral stairs and broke her little neck. — *That* Miss Smith."

Good local stories, being useful, prove humanly durable. They need not travel. They remain a dogged form of exotic half-news. Along today's side street, Mohawked skateboarders retrace pavement slopes found first by deer then ceded to Indian foot traffic relenting to English-bred horses giving way to Henry Ford's presumptuous free-lance buggies. And us. But the future? Overrated. Our local vision of the future? "Nouveau," and too showy by half.

Shouldn't I resent the dead? Shouldn't we resist any club so ready to take in the likes of us? I don't, though. Our dead outnumber us, majority rules.

12.

I planned a party for two hundred or so. My history-minded folks would be its guests of honor. I mailed no invitations. I simply invited friends whenever I met them on the street, in stores. First houseguests, my parents, arrived. I saw at once my mother was not well. The distance from the airport gate to my waiting station wagon seemed a marathon for her. She admitted she should've stayed home but, being middle class, nonrefundable tickets made their coming anyway essential. Though I saw that she was rickety, I did give them the short tour of the finished house.

She had bought a new party dress, unusual for someone who hated shopping. The morning of our housewarming fête, Father and I sat in my breakfast nook. He held a mug of tea before him. Mother had splurged by staying in bed late. At 8 AM we heard her coming down the central staircase. She wore low heels and we both half-smiled at the sound of her approach. My father and I usually exhausted acceptable topics rather quickly. Mom often appeared with neutral reinforcements just in time. I remember looking direct into the saturated blue of my father's eyes when we both heard her fall. (She had been carrying her camera and her purse. Instead of letting a $200 camera topple, she fought for it, releasing the banister.) Down the stairs she came making a sound so solid and sickening I can hardly describe it fifteen years later.

Adrenaline slows things down. That's how it helps us make life-saving decisions. But adrenaline sped up my eyesight. Panic let me see my father set down his mug so quickly, one organized cylinder of hot tea rested steaming above it. Then it all dripped over Dad's hand and lap. He rushed to the sink for a cloth, obsessed with cleaning up. Terror kept him from her side. He already knew.

I found her on her back at the bottom of my almost-grand staircase. (All my pride of possession turned to instant cringing, pure accountability, my fault, my floor wax, my bachelor pretensions to a place this size.) Mother held onto her precious patent-leather purse; she just looked up at me. Vast amounts of information passed between us. "Bruised, yes, undignified, yes. But nothing's broken," she asserted from the floor, flat on her back.

Being a Boy Scout, fearful to move her, I ran for pillows I might at least place under her head. She looked wretched, fully dressed on my bare floor. As I bent beside her, intent on making her comfortable, both of us heard Dad still cleaning up spilt tea. I moved to lift her head. The face below mine, at this slight vexing of her spine, fragmented into scraps and tags and pellets of such agony. We both understood.

Here were my first houseguests, the honored center of tonight's party. Father finally exited the kitchen, drying his hands on a tea towel, feigning indifference while himself hardly able to stay standing. I carried the phone to a far room, dialed 911. Next I called a retired doctor friend. It was 8:30 AM but he sounded unsurprised to hear me. He started in at once about looking forward to tonight's festivities.

"Jack? Listen. My mom has just fallen down my stairs. Think she's broken her hip. Just called the ambulance. Which hospital should we take her to?"

"Durham Regional," he answered. Then, pausing, this most sociable of men, asked, "Does this mean there's no party?"

"Fraid so."

Her fall would effectively end both my parents' lives. Dad would spend his next year, and all his remaining strength, nursing her. He would rush her home from the hospital, bypassing her physical therapy, taking on all the work himself. It proved beyond his strength. And once he died, she would see little reason to continue. There was—aside from her limp and the ugly omnipresent aluminum walker—nothing much wrong with her. Past age, past losing interest, past willingly forfeiting her place on earth.

The fall had happened right here in the home I'd somehow prepared for them, half-dedicated to them. I knew that whatever dollars they might leave me I'd spend chipping away at the mortgage. Her fall made me consider selling the place. I had tried creating a temple to some odd kind of family honor and, one day in, it proved my parents' downfall.

Welcome to human history! By now, from here in time, I see this disaster—like the epidemic that brought me here—as one more bit of the place's truth and my own. Wasn't it better that she fell at my home here, and not in some discount mall's parking lot? A therapist friend would later explain, "Your mother fell at your house because she wanted to die in your company." Eventually, it was in my company she did die. I was there with my youngest brother and she knew we were with her and that made it easier for all of us.

But Mother died in a "Home," not in my own. Home.

I had offered her shelter. I said it would be easy, even fun, to turn my big sunny writing studio into a first-floor bedroom for her. We could bring in a nurse and some high-tech hospital bed. Potted palms, folding screens. I could pretty the place up.

To this she replied, with certainty and sassiness and a smartness that makes me go on loving her, "Son, I'm afraid having me in the middle of your writing-room might be the end of our friendship."

Who could not love such a woman?

She never blamed the house. Or history.

Or me.

13.

I came here to escape the memories of dead young friends only to make new **old** ones. I came to know, as personalities, certain locals dead three hundred years. I find that small cemetery next door far nicer than those huge awful ones in Queens.

I observe and respect village happenings. I daily speak the names of beloved living folks who hail from its three major races. I know my own home's minor role in this town's long tale. Being the nominal owner of this house, I am really just the latest name scratched onto her dance-card.

I sense my own trivial but real part while I'm still actively imaginatively alive here. My time on earth seems, so far, as educational and history-minded as a well-planned two-week vacation.

I suspect I am mortal. No, I "know" that now. I'll be among this village's deceased—perhaps even among its more **likeable** deceased.

Something about living in sight of stones that stand for persons expired these two and a half centuries, it's . . . restful.

Epidemic drove me from the city. I found myself re-grounded here, refined. History here is local, familial, international, natural, completely mine, utterly impersonal.

I know too little. But I study everyday.

This is so much yet to understand.

I see it as a sort of task.

By two parents, now deceased, I was so well-trained for it.

If 109 seems young yet for a home so solidly built, can 62 be all that old for its latest occupant?

I know what a story is.

I can still pay the property taxes.

The house is better for my having found it.

I feel more myself since it somehow took me in.

I live here now.

ALLAN GURGANUS is the author of *Oldest Living Confederate Widow Tells All* (Vintage) — which was on the *New York Times* bestseller list for eight months and has been adapted (by the author and Jane Holding) for the stage. His other books include *Plays Well With Others*, *White People*, and *The Practical Heart* (all published by Vintage). He is recipient of a Guggenheim fellowship and is a member of the American Academy of Arts and Letters. His novel-in-progress is *The Erotic History of the Southern Baptist Church*.

To the Eno

An excerpt from Barefoot to Avalon: a memoir

DAVID PAYNE

WE ARE GOING TO THE ENO, I am with the children, and on the drive, Will, who's seven, tells us a dream about a "War Cat." He finds this creature in a tree trunk near Cameron Park, his school, and brings it home, and I tell him it can't live here. He tries putting it in our real cat's cage, but it picks the lock, and as he tells us this, Will grins a familiar grin—the one of happy illegality—and for a moment in the rearview mirror my son looks like my brother, dead these six years now.

—I had one about a demon, says Grace, his nine-year-old big sister. It came out of a pipe, and Will wanted a Bionicle for his birthday, and the demon let him have it.

—Sounds like a nice demon.

—It was the good kind that likes human beings and grants wishes.

And I tell them that in dreams when things come out of pipes and tree trunks or up from caves or basements, the dream is showing us something that's inside us, maybe not a war cat or a demon, but something war-cat- or demon-like that helps us fight and gain our needs and wishes.

—I have something like that in me, too, I say, and when I write I ask it questions and it answers, and this is what I think people meant a long time ago when they talked about gods and spirits. We once knew more about these things but then decided they were superstitions, and now few people remember them or pay attention. I think it's important, though, and I pay attention, and I hope you'll grow up to pay attention also.

They are quiet over this, and then Will says, I think you are a wise man, Dad.

And I laugh and say, Wiser than last year. . . . How could I not be, with such wise children to instruct me?

And we are on the path now, walking along the ridge and down the switchback that leads us to the water, where the old sycamores, pale white and green, remind me of the ones in Paris. As we go, the dazzle on the water incandesces as the wind roughs it and passes, and the trees toss their heads like stallions and a leaf falls, as green as all the others in the forest, it drops into the water and I think about my brother who once upon a time was as tall and strong as I was.

We put our packs down on a gravel spit the kids call Treasure Island, and Grace with her keen eye says, Dad, come here, come look! And on a big rock in the middle of the river is a snake, a black one with a yellow streak running lengthwise down its belly, and when we peer closely, we see a young one curled up with it, and we watch them sunning, and Will says, Can I poke it? and I say, No, sir, if you poke the snake what does the snake do?

—Bite you?

—Do you want the snake to bite you?

—No way!

—Then find another way to use your energy, Mein War Cat!

And the War Cat and his demon sister splash off laughing toward the chute where the whitewater rushes between two seal-black rocks and ushers into an amber pool that's clear and four or five feet deep in the middle of the river. Beyond lies Treasure Island, which they named when they were younger, and I climb on the rock with the mother snake and snakelet, and the cool breeze and the water have a trace of winter chill still in them, but the sun is warm upon our bodies and casts a dazzle on the honey-colored water and the ancient sycamores, pale green and white, toss their heads like stallions.

Oh, something is changing, something is changing, and here we are, down by the river, here I am with my children, they are in the water and I'm in the water right beside them, and though a snake is sunning with its hatchling not far away I feel no danger for they're warmed by the same sun that I am.

And Grace, our naturalist—who developed her keen eye in Vermont when she was less than two and we walked on the wooded slopes of Northeast Mountain and sought the orange newts she had no fear of—now, from the shallows she brings me gifts of tiny clamshells smaller than an infant's fingernails and says she'd like to make a necklace, and Will on Treasure Island is going, Arrr, me maties! and brandishing the saber of a fallen tree limb sent him by the river or perhaps the mother snake because he spared her and her hatchling. And they are laughing, leaving me, going on their expeditions, riding the chute between the seal-black rocks and returning to me over and over, where I sit on my rock in the middle of the river. They are touching me, my children, putting their thin, chilly arms, all goose-bumps, around me, around my waist and neck and shoulders, and I smell them, smell their hair and skin discreetly as they touch me, hungry for my children, who are hungry for their father and are sitting on my knee and slipping in between my legs and leaning on my shoulder, bringing me their treasures which they lay before me on the rock like tribute to receive my admiration which I give them. And here deep in the woods I think we are coming out of them, here in the middle of the river, we are on a rock like the researcher in my dream who's on the height observing and also in the water, as we are in the water, my children are, and I'm in the water with them, but the water is a good place, and being in the water with them is a good thing, though I am also sitting on this rock and watching, the Watcher watching, the Under-stander, who has no higher ground and wishes none, standing under to support them.

And oh something is changing, something is changing, something has changed in me already. And some day in the future when you're walking on the beach or somewhere by the water and you find this message in the bottle which I wrote in blood and threw into the river trusting it would take it to the ocean and the waves would wash it to you, know I loved you and your mother loved you, know we loved each other also and were fellow travelers and lost our way but having lost our way we struggled through until we found it, and know because we did, that you will, when you are lost and disappointed and cannot help yourself look inward and call out and something deep inside will rise up from a tree trunk or a sewer pipe or it will break three stories up like the light from a rose window to help you as it rose to help your father on his journey in the time I walked beside you. Know what joy I took in you and hold me in remembrance as you hold your mother, remember what we gave you and also how we harmed you, tell the truth in love and spare us absolutely nothing, pin the white rose on your breast on Easter Sunday, pin it with a straight pin beaded with dark green, and walk beyond us on your own adventures.

DAVID PAYNE is the author of five novels, including *Back to Wando Passo, Ruin Creek*, and *Confessions of a Taoist on Wall Street*, which received the Houghton Mifflin Literary Fellowship Award. The current writer-in-residence at Hollins University, David Payne has taught at Bennington and Duke, and is a core member of the MFA Creative Writing Faculty at Queens University of Charlotte. His forthcoming memoir, *Barefoot to Avalon*, concerns his relationship with his brother.

Views of the Eno

BEVERLY A. SCARLETT

THE ENO RIVER IS BEAUTIFUL TODAY. It is high and its waters move swiftly, quietly, yet ever so gently. The deep gray color of the water contrasts with the vibrant fall foliage—ruby red, golden yellow, and shimmering bronze. I love the Eno River, its natural hewn ledges, its exotic wildlife, and its storied people. The Eno River brought life to Hillsborough and Hillsborough's life springs from the Eno.

I haven't always found beauty in this river, or in Hillsborough. I grew up on the outskirts of town during the late sixties and early seventies. My parents were farmers and we worked land along the river. The marshy bottom was my father's chosen place for tobacco plant beds. It wasn't uncommon for him to throw in a few watermelon seeds along the sides. As a child, I considered the Eno to be synonymous with hard labor, long hours of pulling tobacco plants and even longer hours of pegging the plants that were improperly set by the planter. The Eno meant getting our 1955 GMC truck stuck in the bottom and watching Daddy pull it out with the tractor. I had no need to see the waters of the Eno. I only saw more work than I could ever hope to get done before I reached the river's edge.

As a child I did not see the beauty of Hillsborough. The town has a rich multiracial history but during my childhood residents were either white or black. Many of the town's white people lived on the "west end," an area generally not visited by blacks. Blacks lived around Central High School (now Hillsborough Elementary) or near Corbin Street.

Roosevelt Warner, the town's premier brick mason, owned the building across the street from the present-day Warner House. The building housed a laundromat, dry cleaner, café, and Mrs. Holman's beauty and tailor shop. This building was the center of activity for the black community. One could go to Warner's, grab a burger and fries, and catch up on the current events while your clothes washed. Any time you went to the laundromat there was always someone you knew there.

Hillsborough's blossoming black community was Fairview. Many blacks left farms in Cedar Grove, Hurdle Mills, and Rougemont to work in Hillsborough's fabric mills and purchase homes built by James Freeland in Fairview, a quiet neighborhood back then. Fairview residents were proud homeowners. Many had manicured lawns before lawn maintenance became fashionable.

Hillsborough expanded quickly. People from the North moved to the area. New businesses opened; some of the older ones closed. And a private school opened that was particularly significant to my family. Carolina Friends School, located in the countryside not far from town, was actively recruiting African American children to attend its summer camp. Party lines buzzed with the news. African American families were intrigued that they were being asked to send their children to a private school summer camp with white children. *Brown v. Board of Education* had been decided. What was there to lose? Wasn't it just a matter of time before the public schools would be forced to integrate?

One morning in early summer Don and Darlene Wells from the Friends School visited my family. They explained the school's mission to my mother and asked if my sisters and I could attend the summer camp. My mother agreed to send us and to invite students who'd come from up North to

54

staff the camp to share a meal in our home. Once a week all summer long Mama cooked a large supper and hosted the students. Fried chicken was always the meat of choice. Vegetables served were succotash made with fresh homegrown lima beans and corn, mustard greens with chow-chow, green beans or corn on the cob. Mama still remembers a young man who couldn't get enough fried chicken or corn on the cob. After dinner we enjoyed Mama's pound cake as we shared stories about African American culture.

As a preschooler, I attended a couple of summer camps at Carolina Friends. There I learned techniques in conflict resolution, finding one's inner peace, and appreciating nature. I canoed, rode horses, and finger-painted. While my world in Hillsborough continued to be defined in black and white, the Friends School offered a glimpse of the array of colors that create the human rainbow. I vividly remember watching an Asian gentleman pick up his children every day. Each afternoon he stood on the stairs at the top of the hill and called the family name. Each afternoon an Asian child, an African American child, and a white child answered his call. As a preschooler, I wasn't sure how that family came to be but I knew there was something special about it.

In the mid-1960s, I was excited to start first grade at Central Elementary. But unbeknown to me, I had entered a separate and unequal public school system. After my summers at Friends School, I was shocked to find that everyone at school looked like me.

The school was neat and clean but the environment was totally different from the one I'd enjoyed at Carolina Friends. Within a matter of days, I learned that this was not a place for peaceful self-discovery, but one of discipline and corporal punishment. Mrs. Fuller, my teacher, was tall and described as being "big boned." One day she wrote several basic addition problems on the chalkboard. I raised my hand and offered to answer. My answer was incorrect, and Mrs. Fuller asked me to hold out my left hand. I did as instructed and she slapped it with her ruler. The lick was so hard that I am still unsure whether I cried from the sound of the ruler hitting my hand or from pain. From that day until I graduated from college, I never again volunteered to answer anything in a classroom setting.

In second grade, I was surprised when my father picked me up early at school one afternoon. That was so unlike him. I got into the car and Daddy drove my older sister and me across Nash Street. As we reached Union Street, he told us to duck down. I did as I was told at first, but being inquisitive, I popped up and peeped out the window as we passed Central High School, where desks and papers were flying out the windows. I didn't understand what was happening.

Later I overheard adults talking about Orange County schools being integrated. Whites were unhappy, and blacks were outright mad, not wanting to lose their sense of culture and identity. This made for tense times. Hillsborough, like many other Southern towns, struggled to identify itself. Jim Crow had ended and Martin Luther King Jr. had been assassinated. Blacks as well as whites wondered, "Where shall we go from here?"

By the time I entered third grade, the schools had been integrated, and I couldn't have been happier. Attending A.L. Stanback (formerly Central High), I had a new best friend, Tamara Moses, who didn't look anything like me. Tamara spent several afternoons at our home. Her mother would pick her up after supper.

I do not have memories of going to Tamara's house. Years later, I asked Mama about this. I now understand that was her way of protecting me: If the play dates occurred in our home, there were fewer opportunities for me to be upset by racially charged comments. I am sure Tamara's mother would not have made comments of that nature, but how could I convince Mama, the descendant of slaves and survivor of the Jim Crow South?

All of Mama's shielding could not protect me from the school bus. By the time I was in the eighth grade, I was usually the only African American on my bus. My older sister drove a school bus; my younger sister rode the elementary school bus. The other African American riders who occasionally rode the bus were two of my cousins. Truancy was not enforced and they didn't attend school regularly.

My bus route was long. Our house was one of the first stops on the route. The bus ride seemed ten times longer than it actually was. Daily, I was teased for having dark skin. I was asked, didn't my mammy put lard in my hair to comb it? I was called the "n" word.

This was the first time I heard the word black used to describe my race in a way that was demeaning and insulting. In the segregated school system the same word was used with a sense of pride. African Americans spoke of "black power," and James Brown sang, "Say it loud, I'm black and I'm proud." Hearing the negative connotations associated with the word when describing race was a lesson in the importance of tone and context. Depending upon my surroundings, black had two totally different meanings, a single word paradox.

One particularly gray afternoon, the school bus started its usual route from school, turning off Orange High School Road onto Highway 70, then left on Churton Street. I sat on the left side of the bus, trying to ignore the usual heckling and racist comments. I looked out the window, wanting to shed tears. Then I saw it: an old white house surrounded by knee-high weeds. The paint was peeling. It looked abandoned.

Something about that house struck me. I didn't know what it was but I knew that I had to see the house again. Each day after that, I made a point of boarding the bus early so that I could get a window seat on the left side. I would stare at the old house as the bus traveled down Churton Street.

I was drawn to a certain spirit about the house. It made me feel good. It didn't matter what was being said to me. The very sight of that old run-down house soothed me. I daydreamed of living there, of how the house would look painted with its yard mowed. My dreams were lively and colorful, but I could not share them. I had never heard of an African American living on the main street in Hillsborough in such a large house. In my dreams this was totally possible. What was it about that house that made me dream so unrealistically?

When I reached high school, I participated in marching band and track and no longer rode the bus in the afternoons. After graduating from high school, I attended college in Raleigh. From there I worked at UNC Hospitals and at UNC School of Medicine. Before leaving the medical school, I attended law school at North Carolina Central University.

During those fifteen years, I matured and created an identity for myself. I didn't frequent downtown Hillsborough. I did not want to be reminded of segregated schools and the constant heckling. Quietly, the old house faded from my memory.

In 1994, after passing the bar exam, I returned to Hillsborough to open a law office on West King Street. One day as I hurried through town, I saw the old house. I actually noticed the side entrance that faces Dickerson Chapel AME Church. A thousand memories flooded my mind. By this time, improvements had been made to the house and it was more beautiful than I ever imagined. I made a point of traveling past the house as often as I could, savoring its beauty. After a long day in court, it gave me a sense of peace, the same kind of serenity it had given me fifteen years earlier.

During the spring of 1999, our family received an invitation to the 49th Annual Whitted Family Reunion. Portia Harris, the daughter of Norfley Whitted, contacted my mother and asked us to attend. Thinking this was a reunion of a distant line of the family, we chose not to attend.

Norfley Whitted was born in 1905. My childhood memories of him are of a rather tall, striking African American, proud and always dressed in the finest attire. He attended college at present-day North Carolina Central University. Mr. Whitted was employed as a radio announcer for WSRC in Durham and hosted a Sunday morning program called "Wings Over Jordan." Mama always tuned in when he was on the air. He had a mellow baritone voice and played a lot of gospel quartet music. Mr. Whitted was one of Mama's chosen role models for us.

Periodically, Mr. Whitted called Mama to catch up on our set of Whitteds. However, most of their catching up took place in Durham at Mechanics and Farmers Bank. What should have been a ten-minute bank transaction turned into a one-hour sidewalk chat for Mama and Mr. Whitted. As a child I wondered why they needed to talk so much. I didn't mind listening to his unique voice and proper English but I got tired of standing there.

One day I asked Mama if she was kin to Mr. Whitted, and she said, "He says so but I didn't hear Papa say anything about it." This was confusing because there were so many African American Whitteds in Hillsborough and Durham. How could so many people of the same race and same last name in the same place not be related?

Depending upon whom you asked, there were five or six different sets of Whitteds in the area. Younger generations of Whitteds were identified by their parents and grandparents. The real mystery was that Whitteds married Whitteds.

As an adult, I continued to ask Mama about the Whitteds. She could not give me the answers I needed. I learned not to ask too many questions. I had been on the receiving end of Mama's backhand and had no intentions of going there again.

In 2004, I received a telephone call from my older sister: "Girl, you will not believe this! I went to Blue Mayo's to get the boys' hair cut. While I was there, he asked me wasn't Mama a Whitted before she married. When I answered yes, he gave me a notebook to read. It is the Whitted family history, and it is so interesting. Can you believe there is a Whitted House in Hillsborough that's on the historic register?"

I asked if it was a white house. She replied yes. I said, "Please don't tell me it is at the corner of Churton and Queen streets." "It sure is." At that point I understood my connection to the old white house.

I reminded my sister of my horrible school bus rides and told her how the house became a sanctuary for me. My sister replied, "You don't know anything yet. You must get a copy of the notebook! Once you've read it you will see that we are connected to that house."

I called Portia Harris and attended two family reunions to learn more about the Whitteds of Hillsborough. It turns out, Norfley Whitted's father had passed down oral history and knew how we are all connected. When Mr. Whitted retired he asked his daughter and granddaughter to do what they could to get the history recorded, an onerous job mainly done by Mr. Whitted's great-granddaughter, Krishna Mayfield, who started documenting the Whitted family history as a high school project. Fortunate to have started collecting information prior to the deaths of her great-grandfather and other known descendants of the original Whitted family, Krishna used these resources to verify information. After years of labor, she presented the notebook, complete with greetings from President Clinton and Governor Jim Hunt, to the Whitted family members at the fiftieth family reunion in 2000.

Finally in January 2008, early on a Saturday morning, I went to Blue Mayo's barbershop and borrowed the family notebook. I started reading it about the time snow began to fall, the first snow Hillsborough had seen in a long time. As I savored the snow, I tried to absorb the beauty and richness of the history of the Whitted family.

Orange County was founded in 1752. At the time the county was formed most of its settlers were German and Irish from Pennsylvania or English. Most made their home along the Eno River where the soil was rich and ripe for planting. Quakers made up a portion of the county's population and settled in the areas of Cane Creek and Stinking Quarter Creek.

Orange County was known for its tolerance. Only 8 percent of the population held slaves. One slaveholding family was the Whitted family who came here around the time that the county was formed. William Whitted Sr. was a Quaker who migrated from Pennsylvania. He had sons named Jehu, Levi, and William Jr.

The African American Whitted oral history tells of Quakers who owned slaves and granted their slaves many freedoms. Several Whitted slaves were taught to read and write. Slaves raised their own crops and shared them, creating a true system of sharecropping. Our oral history tells of slaves who were able to write their own passes and moved about the county freely. Many owned their own blacksmithing tools and worked privately to support their families.

Credibility is given to the oral history of the African American Whitteds by the WPA (Works Progress Administration) interview of Anderson Whitted in 1937. (This interview is online.) Credibility is further established by facts contained in the wills of the original Whitted men. (The wills are online, and the originals are recorded in the Estates Division of the Orange County Clerk of Superior Court.) The will of William Whitted Sr. provided for the emancipation of his mulatto boy Dick in the year 1820. William Whitted Jr. was the executor of his father's will. William Jr.'s will acknowledged his father's desire to emancipate Dick. However William Jr. loaned Dick out to Thomas Holden and provided for his emancipation following this indenture.

Jehu Whitted's will provided for the emancipation of the mulatto child, Fanny, daughter of Hetty. Jehu's executor was instructed to use all lawful means to bring that about. Jehu requested that his father, William Whitted Sr., and his brother William Jr. be granted a hundred pounds of current money to be held in trust for Fanny. Further, Jehu provided that she be given a basic education and should not suffer to be removed from Orange County.

When I turned twenty-one, my mother told me about her Grandpa Dick Whitted, the mulatto from William Sr.'s will. Although he had died before Mama was born, Grandpa Dick was often the subject of conversation in her parents' home. Mama mentioned that Grandpa Dick was biracial but that was not to be talked about. She showed us the old log cabin he had owned and had shared with my grandparents when they married. Eventually, they built their own home. After Grandpa Dick passed away, his cabin was used as the kitchen. It was common in the early 1900s to have the kitchen separated from the main house.

Grandpa Dick owned property in the Saint Mary's area of Hillsborough. When his son, my mother's father, Page, reached the age of ten, Grandpa Dick took him into his home and raised him. Grandpa Dick left his daughter with his children's mother. As unusual as this arrangement is by today's standards, it worked. Mama knew that her branch of the Whitted family was much smaller than the others, and she had no idea how Grandpa Dick got property in Saint Mary's.

Reading the Whitted family history I learned that all the area's African American Whitteds are connected by and to the original white Quaker Whitted family of Hillsborough. Yes, there are many sets of us and Whitteds can legally marry other Whitteds. My set of Whitteds lost its connection to other African American Whitteds generations ago, when Grandpa Dick was loaned to Thomas Holden.

From my own research I learned that Thomas Holden owned land in the Saint Mary's area of Hillsborough. I believe that once Grandpa Dick was freed, he did not reunite with the other Whitteds but chose to stay near Thomas Holden and make Saint Mary's his home. (Other research revealed that Thomas Holden and a few members of the original Whitteds are interred in a family cemetery at the corner of Saint Mary's Road and Dumont Drive.)

The family history as documented by Krishna Mayfield sheds light on the many contributions African American Whitteds made to this area:

James E. Shepard, founder of North Carolina Central University.

James Whitted, namesake of Whitted School in Durham.

Milton Toby Fitch, Jr., Superior Court Judge; former State
 Representative; Masonic grandmaster.

London Whitted, principal of the Quaker Normal School and first
 African American principal in Orange County.

Richard Whitted, Orange County Commissioner.

Clyde Whitted, Hillsborough Historian.

Alice Whitted, employee of the MacNider family of UNC's Medical
 School and honoree of the library at Frank Porter Graham
 Elementary School.

The richness of the history of Orange County and the entire Whitted family has removed the gray one-dimensional lens from my view. I am able to appreciate what it means to respect and accept all aspects of my heritage. What began as a journey of a poor second-class citizen has evolved to a rich experience of discovery.

While many may consider a slaveholding family history as part of a painful past that should be forgotten, I consider the Whitted history a story of tolerance, hard work, and unity. I am proud to be born and raised and now raising a new generation along the banks of the Eno River in a town with a past and present that are both wonderful and complicated.

I view Hillsborough as the place of my identity, the place where I was restrained, the place where I was set free, the place where I discovered me.

BEVERLY SCARLETT is a Hillsborough native and the first African American woman to serve as a judge in Judicial District 15-B (Orange and Chatham counties). She also is only the third judge from the northern part of Orange County to serve the district since Reconstruction.

Settling In

PETER H. WOOD

"LOOK, THERE'S A FOR SALE SIGN." It was 1975, and I had been house-hunting in Hillsborough for half an hour, driving the leafy streets with another American historian, a friend from Chapel Hill. I had just taken a job teaching early American history at Duke. "If I am going to move to North Carolina," I said, "it makes sense to live in a town that has visible eighteenth-century roots."

I noticed the wide swing on the front porch almost as soon as I saw the hand-lettered "For Sale" yard sign swaying in the spring breeze. The small gray house, built shortly after World War I, had been fixed up a decade earlier by a young architect; he had installed new wiring, added antique "tear drops" to the porch pillars, and built a staircase in the front hall that converted the attic into a bedroom loft.

The current occupants were leaving the Triangle to take environmental jobs elsewhere, and the asking price amazed me. I had just spent three years working in grimy, expensive New York and Boston. Let's just say that the bill for replacing the porch and the front walk twenty-five years later came to almost as much as they were asking for the whole house. I made a down payment that afternoon and headed north to pack.

In May I rattled south in my green Dodge van to take up residence in Orange County. It was almost dark when I arrived, so I strolled down to the Minnis family grocery on West King Street to stock up on a few supplies. When Mrs. Minnis told me that their freshman son was just starting Duke too, I said, "Nice, is he a little nervous?" She cocked her head and paused to think it over. "Not nearly as nervous as you are," she replied.

Bingo. I had sauntered into the store in blue jeans and work shoes, feeling specially relaxed, but clearly I still seemed a bit too revved up. I recognized this cautionary form of greeting from other small towns where I had spent time, in South Carolina and Maine. It was just the reminder I needed. One thing that had drawn me to the South, past and present, was the slower pace of time.

As I walked home to unpack, I recalled my plan to buy a rocker for the front porch. Thanks to Mrs. Minnis, it moved to the top of my to-do list, even though I was healthy, busy, and still only in my early thirties. The next morning, I stepped out the kitchen door to survey my new surroundings. A beautiful magnolia tree blossomed in my neighbor's yard; a mockingbird, perched on a high branch, was singing its heart out. I laughed out loud to see a Southern myth become my backyard reality.

Classes began in Durham the next week, and sometime the next month I walked into a law office on Churton Street. The lady greeting me explained that the lawyer had gone to lunch, but I was welcome to wait. "No thanks, I'll try again," I said. "I need to go into town." She gave me a look not too different from the one I had received in the Minnis grocery. Then in a motherly tone, as if correcting a child who is temporarily lost or mixed up, she reminded me, "You're already *in town*."

Affordable real estate, a leisurely pace, and a strong sense of small town pride were not the only things I noticed as I adapted happily to Hillsborough in the mid-seventies. Hillsborough was also adapting to people

66

like me, wondering how many more newcomers would lack the warm Carolina drawl that Senator Sam Ervin had shared with the country in the recent Watergate Hearings. Who were these strangers who seemed to view the county seat, once the largest village in the Piedmont, as a bedroom community?

More importantly, would newcomers like me reinforce, or undermine, the long-standing hierarchies and accepted "ways"? After all, I still had Massachusetts plates on my van, so I was only briefly surprised when a policeman pulled me over for a "rolling stop" at the intersection a block from my house. It was clear that he just wanted to check out who I was; unfamiliar vehicles were as uncommon as unfamiliar faces and accents.

Nor did it stop there. Within a week, I received a phone call from someone who said in a threatening voice, "Just want to let you know that we know yer here, and we're watchin' you." This seemed almost as jarringly stereotypical as the mockingbird in the magnolia, but less easy to smile about. A month later somebody lobbed an egg against the front of the house. If I felt duly threatened, obviously others felt threatened too.

The local gun shop on Churton Street still had an emblematic Confederate flag sticker on the front window, and a few years after that phone call, the Ku Klux Klan got a permit to march through town. But time, even if it moved slowly, was heading in a different direction. I bought my North Carolina license plates, and there were no more raw eggs. I read in the paper that at recently integrated Orange High, students resolved one thorny debate temporarily by agreeing to elect a white and a black homecoming queen.

No one helped me settle in more than Annie Lockhart, the kindly widow next door. She had come to town to teach school after World War I, when a train still stopped in Hillsborough every day. She married a local bank manager, and they built a home on North Wake Street, planting a little pecan tree in the backyard that later towered over the house.

Mrs. Lockhart kept a small bust of Beethoven on the piano in the front parlor, where she gave music lessons to several generations of Hillsborough children. When her own children were young, the street remained a dirt road, almost as it had been in Revolutionary times. She remembered the excitement and the sticky feet when Wake Street got a tar surface during the Great Depression. Later, children unwittingly rode their bicycles close behind the large truck that sprayed DDT to kill mosquitoes.

Of course, Mrs. Lockhart was interested in her new neighbor. Though she lived alone, she was a key part of various local grapevines, and she wanted to learn all about me. It wasn't hard. She would call from her porch, "Dr. Wo-od," in her musical Piedmont voice, "Dr. Wo-od, I've baked you a peach pie."

With the very first of these delicious pies, or maybe the second, I was invited in to chat and look at the family scrapbook. Her son had been one of the first Americans wounded in Britain during World War II, and the Queen of England had visited his bedside. For Mrs. Lockhart that huge honor seemed to more than offset what turned out to be a small wound.

I had little to offer in return for what came out of the old oven in Mrs. Lockhart's kitchen. But she knew I was teaching Southern history and asked if she could see the book I had written. It dealt with slavery in early South Carolina, and the cover featured a painting of a handsome black man, under the title, *Black Majority*. The book told a grim story about how the Carolinas came to be. Needless to say, there were no magnolia trees in the moonlight. I realized that it might not be her particular cup of tea, but, having no alternative, I shared a copy.

About ten days later, Mrs. Lockhart called me on the phone. Clearly this was something too serious to discuss from porch to porch. "Dr. Wo-od," she said, "I've read all through that book of yours, and I have found out the most interesting thing." I braced myself—no more peach pies—and asked what that might be. "Why," she replied with pleasure and triumph in her voice, "I found out *how old you are!*"

Fair enough. As I tell my students, read with a purpose. Always figure out who wrote a book, checking the dust jacket for information before you try to gauge what the author has to say.

Did someone in her Hillsborough networks assign Annie Lockhart the task of discretely checking out the newcomer next door? Or did she simply take it on herself in a combination of kindliness and inquisitiveness? I shall never know, but she performed her duties like someone from an Agatha Christie novel. I have always been grateful that she gave me passing marks and assisted my settling in. I still stop at her grave when I visit the Town Cemetery off of East Corbin Street.

PETER H. WOOD was born in St. Louis and raised in Baltimore before moving to Hillsborough. He taught early American history at Duke for thirty-two years and retired recently to grow gourds and write books. He is the co-author of a U.S. history survey entitled *Created Equal*, plus several books on the American artist, Winslow Homer.

Street Scenes

Identity Crisis

BOB BURTMAN

A CAUTIONARY NOTE in Hillsborough's sweet symphony: The town has evolved into its present, vital self as much by accident as design, shielded from the ravages of growth and homogenization by a confluence of circumstances that had more to do with luck than intent, like a turtle that manages to cross the interstate and finds itself in a reptilian Shangri-La.

What Hillsborough offers is by no means unique, though it has become increasingly hard to find. Even first-time visitors intuitively grasp the sense of place that defines the town. In Hillsborough, the components of place—history, architecture, topography, culture, people—interconnect in a powerful, even palpable way. Call it community, though that term has lost much of its meaning in a virtual age of Balkanized subcultures and micro-interests. There's a better word: identity.

The components that comprise identity exist everywhere, but in much of the United States they've become fragmented and dissociated from each other. In that respect, Hillsborough less resembles a contemporary American town than a venerable European village or rural New England borough, where personal identity is inseparably intertwined with place, and where the collective desire to preserve local identity and build upon its foundation is the epoxy that binds everything together.

What sets Hillsborough apart from similarly rooted burgs that have been around for a couple of centuries is the pace and direction of change in recent years. The town has officially been on the map since 1766, a typical, sleepy North Carolina whistle stop for the bulk of its existence, run by a succession of small-pond big fish who were born and raised within a few miles of the courthouse. In the early 1970s, many of the downtown storefronts were vacant and remained that way off and on for more than two decades, as the surviving retailers hobbled along, one cavernous Tyrannostore away from the grave.

The Tyrannostore finally came in 2003 (and another one shortly after that), but by then the town had gone retro, back to a time when residents traded with downtown merchants as a matter of course, when hometown pride meant more than a championship high school sports team or a local boy made good, where people hit the streets at all hours, engaged. The people whose aggregate vision had transformed Hillsborough, the old-timers who weathered the static times alongside the transplants who had moved there partly on faith, had somehow monkey-wrenched the malevolent machinery of progress.

Hillsborough residents aren't in political or ideological lockstep, but the one point on which they seem to universally agree is that they've got something worth holding on to. The unnaturally compressed timeframe of the town's reinvention, however, suggests that as quickly as Hillsborough gained its fresh identity, it can morph back into Anywhereville just as fast.

For a nation that prides itself on embodying the spirit of rugged individualism, Americans have become a hopelessly conformist lot. Nowhere is this evidenced more vividly than in our suburban and exurban landscapes, where once-distinctive small cities and towns have become virtually indistinguishable from one another. The sense of place that grounded residents in their communities has disappeared in a sterile sea of shopping malls and cloned subdivisions, where neighbors don't know each other's names and deviations from the Approved Norm constitute grounds for eviction.

The Triangle area of North Carolina, at least the bulk of it, has not escaped this fate. Its three points, Raleigh, Durham, and Chapel Hill, have expanded exponentially in size the last three decades as people migrated in droves from less hospitable regions, attracted by the abundance of jobs, moderate clime, and low cost of living. Cary, which in the early 1970s had a population roughly equivalent to Hillsborough's today, became the area's bedroom destination and now has more than 100,000 residents — a twenty-fold increase.

The new residents sought to transplant not just themselves but the familiar trappings of modern culture, erecting prefab fortresses in prefab PUDs (Planned Unit Developments) next to prefab shopping clusters, bulldozing the discomfiting vestiges of the past and replacing them with anti-septic facsimiles. Politicians willingly abetted this wholesale modification under the banner of economic development. Landowners whose property had been in their families for generations sold out, speculators cashed in.

The frenetic pace of growth inexorably altered or destroyed the funda-mental character of cities and towns throughout the Triangle, sweeping in every direction and metastasizing like a malignant tumor. Hillsborough has bucked this trend, though to say "bucked" is misleading, as it implies a conscious series of actions and a common purpose that have guided the town's destiny. In fact, Hillsborough's fortunes have largely rested on forces beyond its control.

As the Triangle entered its period of interstellar growth, Hillsborough should have been a likely target for the flood of refugees and the parasites who attended them. Land and historic downtown properties were relatively cheap with no shortage of willing sellers. The attitude of town officials could be summarized as "we'll take anything we can get." The proximity to two interstate highways and easy access to the Research Triangle Park employment hub offered the perfect suburban commute.

But two primary factors steered development elsewhere. The first was a matter of reputation—not Hillsborough's, but Durham's. The city that sits between Hillsborough and the Triangle's axis was perceived in some circles as a dangerous hellhole of crime and poverty—largely due to its large, politically active black population—that evoked the worst fears of the new arrivals. Durham's notoriety, which persists to this day, was famously fueled by real estate agents who steered prospective homebuyers to Cary and other allegedly safer locales.

Hillsborough, hidden behind Durham from the rest of the Triangle like a moon in eclipse, never registered on the development radar screen, even as the area's construction boom reached its peak in the late 1980s and 1990s.

Many immigrants did find their way to Chapel Hill, which like Hillsborough is located in Orange County and is home to the University of North Carolina's flagship campus. A classic college town with high property values, Chapel Hill features the usual cultural amenities in a small-town environment. Chapel Hill also has a highly regarded public school system that has long been a deciding factor for relocating families willing to pay a premium for a top-notch education.

Hillsborough, however, is in a separate county school system, a relic of the dual city-county structure that used to be the norm in North Carolina but gradually has given way elsewhere to unified school districts. The Orange County system, though ranking favorably among school districts in the state, was nevertheless perceived as second-rate in comparison. So while Hillsborough would have been a natural spillover option for those who preferred to live in a less urban area like Chapel Hill, relatively few ventured across district lines.

Hillsborough has now generated sufficient buzz as a premier place to live in the Triangle to overcome those barriers. But a key obstacle to growth remains: the lack of water. Even with the construction of a new reservoir in the 1990s, the town's water capacity will be maxed out with the approval of just a few major projects. While the use of wells could permit some larger-scale development outside town limits, the constricted water supply coupled with the exorbitant cost of expanding it means that Hillsborough will remain close to its present size by default for the foreseeable future.

Lucky breaks all, and those weren't the only ones. In 2003, town planners were caught with their pants down when an asphalt plant operator filed a permit application to build a plant within spitting distance of downtown. The town maneuvered to block the plant, even though the property was zoned for that use. The plant was never built, but a lawsuit by the operator resulted in four years of hand-wringing and a hefty payout by the town.

To be sure, Hillsborough benefited from the foresight of at least a few citizens over the years, in particular the preservationist crowd whose efforts helped save most of the historic buildings in town. But blocking the pillagers from doing to Hillsborough as they did to Cary would have been like holding off the Huns with a handful of pitchforks, a futile exercise without Fortuna's divine intervention.

The price of success is eternal vigilance. As more people discover the benefits and pleasures of old-school living, Hillsborough faces numerous pressures that threaten to undermine its identity. The debilitating process of gentrification has already begun—while not yet epidemic, the specter of older and lower-income residents being pushed out of town, their modest homes replaced by lot-filling monstrosities, is a familiar one across the country. The retention and construction of affordable housing are but two of many ways to ensure the town's cultural and economic diversity.

That diversity, an essential part of Hillsborough's identity, goes beyond the usual race and sex categories. What might be called New South and

Old South not only coexist, atypical in a region where rapid growth and the influx of outsiders have often fomented cultural clashes, but each appreciates the value the other brings to the table. The ability of creative types to survive and thrive in the town has added immeasurably to the cultural mix. And while many small towns have lost their kids to the city and are aging into extinction, Hillsborough is multigenerational and infused with youth energy. Maintaining that balance poses challenges with no easy solutions.

The current crop of town and county officials understands that it can proactively protect Hillsborough's identity and operate from a position of strength, rather than accepting whatever comes along with a dollar sign attached. Recently, the town board turned down a proposal by a Raleigh outfit to build a cookie-cutter mixed-use development on the massive Daniel Boone tract along South Churton Street, a key cog in Hillsborough's long-range plan. The outcome, which raised few objections and would have been quite different but a decade ago, provided the clearest indication to date that Hillsborough residents are philosophically in sync regarding the town's future.

But one bad election cycle can alter that reality overnight, as happened in neighboring Chatham County. In 2002, a car-wash magnate and his allies unseated the preservationist-minded majority on the Chatham Board of Commissioners and opened the floodgates to massive subdivision projects, permanently altering the landscape as well as the county's rural character. County voters rectified the mistake two years later, but it was too late to undo the damage wrought across Chatham, the large swaths of barren asphalt and acres of denuded forest that still blight the terrain.

Americans have embraced transience as a kind of lifestyle, cutting themselves off from place and community, secure in the false promise of instant resurrection at the next destination. Some are fortunate enough to find home again, but most never do. The consequences of losing our place in the world are isolation, alienation, and fear—traits on full display among the masses, flashing relentlessly like Las Vegas neon, visible to all but the blind.

Hillsborough, contrarian in trumpeting the value of place, has withstood hurricane-force winds that have pushed the Triangle toward identity oblivion. Here's hoping the same can be said down the road.

BOB BURTMAN is a freelance investigative reporter and researcher who lives with his wife and critters in the woods outside Hillsborough. A former staff writer for the *Houston Press*, he has won numerous national and regional awards for his work on the environment, criminal justice, and government corruption. He also hosts a music show, "Roots Rampage," on community radio station WCOM in Carrboro.

Hillsborough in Time & Space

A View From Afar

THOMAS J. CAMPANELLA

THERE COMES A PASSAGE in every person's life when the fulcrum between past and future subtly shifts, when the hoard of spent years, graced with a patina of time, begins to define or even outweigh one's hope for coming things. We begin to treasure the past as we sense the limits of life, to understand our own mortality. Our nostalgia for the past is inversely proportional to our stock in the future. A child has little or no sense of history; the future is all. To an elder the past holds life's treasure.

And so too with nations and cultures. The arc of human society through time mirrors that of an individual's life—from strapping youth to the measured years of adulthood, to eventual superannuation and decline. In each stage, a society values its own history differently, from youth's dismissal of all things old, to age's often-obsessive preoccupation with artifacts of youthful days. One discards the priceless; the other prizes rubbish.

Corollary to this is the fact that a love of the past—senephilia, for lack of a better term—is a function of affluence and arrival. The poor do not, generally, found historical societies; more urgent matters fill their days. It is only after we (individuals as well as societies) achieve a certain threshold level of material comfort and security that we can afford to steward our own history. The past also gains appeal as it recedes, the distance enabling us to overlook just how violent, hungry, filthy, unjust, miserable, and brief life yesterday often was.

The allure of history is thus, paradoxically, conditional upon forgetting much of it. Stewardship of the past is also often editorial, a snipping of the whole-cloth of history to omit unsavory bits and leave only that which flatters the editor. The fallen scraps may well reveal more about us as a people and a culture than the swatches so carefully chosen.

My wife and I have spent the last few years shuttling between two very different places—Hillsborough, North Carolina, and Nanjing, China, where one of us teaches architecture part of the year. We have a small apartment in a neighborhood near Nanjing University with as many residents as all of Hillsborough (Nanjing itself—a smallish city in China—has a population equal to the state of North Carolina).

Moving between Hillsborough and Nanjing is a passage between worlds, and not only for the obvious reasons of language or ethnicity or even scale. It has more to do with vastly different values regarding heritage, history, preservation, and development.

Until only recently, visiting China was effectively a return to the past. Decades of Maoism had plunged the nation into a time warp, its regression dramatized by the spectacular ascent of neighbors like Singapore, Hong Kong, and South Korea in the 1970s. When I first visited the People's Republic in 1992, steam locomotives were still widely in use. Private automobiles were rare, and there were less than a hundred miles of modern, high-speed motorway in the entire country. Shanghai had two modern, high-rise office buildings, neither of which was very tall. Cell phones and personal computers were unheard of.

Today, of course, China is a nation literally and figuratively on the rise. No nation has ever built more than China has in the last thirty years; none has lifted more people out of poverty. Now home to the largest shopping malls, theme parks, car dealerships, and gated communities on earth, China boasts the longest bridges in the world, the biggest airport, half the world's ten tallest buildings (one of which now looms over our Nanjing apartment). Shanghai has twice as many skyscrapers as New York City. Bicycles are being displaced by luxury sedans and SUVs. By 2020 China will have more miles of highway than the United States.

To visit China today is to drink from the proverbial firehose, to come face to face with a future no longer being principally authored by us. It is also to see ourselves as we once were—reckless, daring, determined to shake the world. The priapic skylines of Shanghai or Guangzhou are not only bar graphs of China's national ego, but proof that the drive and ambition that once defined America have found a new home. China makes us painfully aware that we are no longer a nation Emerson called "the country of the future . . . of beginnings, of projects, of vast designs and expectations."[1]

China makes us old. To come home from China is to alight from a bullet train, its turbine scream ringing in your ears.

The relative youth or age of a society determines how it values its heritage; and clearly the United States and China are at vastly different points on that arc. We think of China as timeless and ancient, and in many ways it is. But it is also a culture whose historical trajectory was artificially interrupted. During the Cultural Revolution, Mao Zedong tried to wipe away all traces of the feudal past, effectively severing China's tendons to its own history. Temples and shrines were defaced; Beijing's 600-year-old walls were razed. At Zhongshan University members of the history faculty

---

[1] Ralph Waldo Emerson, "The Young American," *The Dial* 4 (April 1844): 492.

were even lynched. The Maoist denigration of history created a kind of collective amnesia in China, diminishing the "street value" of its own past.

China is a society newly reborn. Today's China—the nation of construction cranes and newly minted millionaires—dates back only to 1978, when Deng Xiaoping ushered in a new era of capitalist enterprise. It is a nation in the flower of youth, obsessed with the new, anxious to compensate for the scarcities and poverty of recent decades. The past in China is thus either a distant memory or too fresh and painful to be cherished. The combination does not make for a nation of preservationists.

Anyone with a love of old buildings will be crushed to see urban China. Seemingly everywhere, the character for "demolish"—chai (拆)—is dashed in paint on the walls of buildings about to be razed. It has become a kind of urbanistic memento mori, the mark of an insatiable modernizing beast. In its headlong rush toward modernity, China has destroyed more neighborhoods—and displaced more urban residents—than any nation in the peacetime history of the world. Urban renewal in Beijing has leveled an area of the city equal in size to most of Manhattan, wiping out neighborhoods two and three times as old as anything in the United States. In Shanghai in the 1990s, an estimated 300 million square feet of old housing was bulldozed for redevelopment. This displaced some 1.8 million people, more than the population of the Research Triangle and nearly twice the number of people uprooted by thirty years of urban renewal in the United States.

If China is an ancient society reborn, hurtling toward the future with nary a backward glance, the United States is a society in tweedy middle age, looking back with increasing wistfulness. The Chinese yearn for the very things Americans now want to be rid of—SUVs and suburban sprawl, big-box superstores, Happy Meals and KFC, life packaged for easy consumption, purged of the pain and hardship of leaner times.

Americans have enjoyed the fruits of affluence for several generations now; we are growing tired of consumerism's empty promises; we want something different. Sick of the simulated and the themed, the franchised and the virtual, we want authenticity, an unmediated engagement with life. We yearn for the very things our grandparents had but our parents threw away—real towns where our kids can walk to school; homes made of honest materials instead of particleboard and resin; chickens and cows with flesh untainted by growth hormones; bicycles and trains and trolleys to move us around.

This longing for the authentic—for an alternative to contemporary consumer culture—also animates our increasing American preoccupation with the past. Yesterday has become a kind of imagined utopia of the genuine, a Thoreauvian world where hale folk lived deeply and sucked at the marrow of life. We want a piece of that past, to remedy our franchised and mass-produced existence. Americans are insatiable consumers of their own heritage. "Antiques Roadshow," appropriately enough an Old-World import, is PBS's highest rated program, attracting some 10 million viewers weekly. "This Old House" is not far behind, syndicated to over 300 stations. Arcadia Publishing has made a fortune with its sepia-tinted Images of America series of local history books. The nearly 4,500 titles, including one on Hillsborough, constitute a national scrapbook of our past.

Of course, American senephilia is itself a relatively new thing. Like China, we too had our love affair with modernity, and cast aside all things old. We bulldozed our cities and built bright Utopias for the motorcar. Heritage preservation came only in fits and starts, and some of the earliest efforts were motivated as much by fear as by altruism. The Colonial Revival movement of the early twentieth century was largely a response to the mass immigration brought by the industrial revolution. Newcomers were seen as a threat by the white, Anglo-Saxon Protestant majority, which reacted by bolstering its claim as the nation's "charter culture."

Greenfield Village, red-brick Georgian architecture, and Colonial Williamsburg were all partly attempts to dial back the cultural clock, or at least remind people who wound it in the first place. It is no coincidence that this was also an era of isolationism, cross burnings, and screeds like Madison Grant's *The Passing of the Great Race* (1916) — a pseudo-scholarly lament on the waning power of northern European peoples. One of the bestsellers of the Jazz Age, the book influenced federal legislation to limit the influx of Jews, Italians, and other ethnic groups deemed a hazard to WASP hegemony.

Grant was also a key figure in the conservation movement. He helped establish several national parks, pioneered the concept of wildlife management, and campaigned to protect the American bison and the California redwoods. He did so not out of love for humanity, but to defend natural wonders he considered as extraordinary—and as endangered—as the Nordic race.

It was not until the 1960s that historic preservation began gaining momentum in the United States. The movement, formed mostly at the grassroots level, was set off by the excesses of urban renewal and by the loss of beloved landmarks, such as New York's Pennsylvania Station. But it was also part of a larger cultural rejection of modernity, of the dehumanizing forces of progress that had come to define America during the Cold War. A generation of youth made their way back to the garden, denouncing bigness and complexity, militarism, and the materialism of American consumer culture—TV dinners and multilane highways, pesticides, the military-industrial complex, the Bomb. Like the concomitant civil rights and environmental movements, preservation activism in this period led to major federal legislation, such as the National Historic Preservation Act of 1966.

Hillsborough was not exactly a center of counterculture activism in the 1960s, but neither was it immune to the larger currents of social change. Just as in New York and San Francisco, Hillsborough made its first real attempt to preserve its architectural heritage during that decade.

By this time Hillsborough was more than 200 years old, with a biography that reads like that of Benjamin Button: an illustrious early history preceded a long period of decline and eventual economic near-abandonment. Hillsborough witnessed some of the opening acts in the American Revolution. It was occupied by British General Cornwallis in 1781, whose troops are said to have laid the town's fieldstone streets. It served as the state capital several times, and had hosted five meetings of the North Carolina General Assembly by 1784. It was in Hillsborough that North Carolinians debated ratification of the federal Constitution (delaying a vote until a Bill of Rights was added).

Though passed over as permanent state capital, Hillsborough remained the seat of Orange County and the center of a flourishing agricultural region up to the Civil War. The Colonial and Antebellum eras left a rich legacy of buildings, crowned by one of the finest Greek Revival courthouses in America. Most of this early stock survived well into the twentieth century. According to local apocrypha, Hillsborough was even a candidate for the period restoration John D. Rockefeller eventually undertook at Williamsburg.

Hillsborough in the 1960s was a typical small Southern town, fractured along lines of race and class. Blacks occupied a separate and unequal world and were largely unwelcome downtown. West Hillsborough was a scrappy mill town with its own culture and economy. Local industry was struggling with increased competition from overseas. Mills began closing or cutting back operations, ravaging the economy and forcing young people to seek greener pastures elsewhere. Others joined the national migration to the suburbs, made easy by an emerging order of highways and motoring.

With ridership plunging, Southern Railway ended passenger service in 1963, taking Hillsborough off the nation's rail grid for the first time since the Civil War. Supermarkets and shopping malls drained customers away from downtown. Construction of a new suburban high school stole away the laughter and bustle of students.

In the face of such problems, stewardship of history was forced to take a back seat to survival. Hillsborough's past was remembered with pride, but aside from a handful of structures salvaged for the Daniel Boone theme park by local entrepreneur James J. Freeland, little was done to preserve its legacy. History had become expendable. Even Occoneechee Mountain, sacred to area Native Americans, was sacrificed for a strip mine.

The tipping point came with the destruction of the legendary Nash-Kollock School on Margaret Lane. Like Pennsylvania Station, its loss galvanized a nascent local preservation movement, and became a catalyst for a new ethic of heritage conservation in town. Leading this grassroots effort was a newcomer to town named Mary Claire Engstrom, a Missouri native and scholar of eighteenth-century English literature. As an affluent outsider, she could afford to see in Hillsborough what Hillsboroughans could not—a sullied but exquisite diamond.

Engstrom founded the Hillsborough Historical Society in 1963, and her survey for the Historic American Building Survey led to the establishment of the Hillsborough Historic District a decade later. However exhaustive, these excavations were not free of Engstrom's own biases. Of patrician stock herself—she was a Randolph on her mother's side—Engstrom was chiefly interested in Hillsborough's genteel past, in the Colonial era and the homes of the largely English early families. She and her husband lived in the grandest of these, the former residence of William Hooper, signer of the Declaration of Independence.

Engstrom had little interest in the town's rich African American legacy or its extraordinary record of Native American settlement. Nevertheless, Engstrom is owed a great debt for effectively rescuing Hillsborough from itself. She even restored the town's old English name, ending more than a century of the vernacular shorthand "Hillsboro."

The establishment of the Historic District primed Hillsborough's future. Ironically, it made the past profitable: Once sacrificed in the name of progress and economic development, history would now become the town's most bankable asset. It would also be a core element of the town's identity; in promotional literature, Hillsborough is almost always modified by "historic."

The Historic District assured newcomers that the qualities that drew them to the town in the first place were bedrock safe. Hillsborough became a sanctuary from the land development maelstrom that, by the 1980s, had engulfed the Triangle and churned much of it into subdivisions and malls. It offered the very values—authenticity, history, density, walkability, a sense of community, a sense of place—that were tossed aside by corporate builders in their rush to make "home" just another commodity for easy consumption. So rare have these qualities of place become that entire upscale developments have been scratch-built to provide them; what are Southern Village or Meadowmont, after all, but clumsy attempts to manufacture the genus loci that Hillsborough has possessed for 250 years?

Implicit in Hillsborough's appeal is a rejection of the dehumanizing sprawl that has come to define so much of the Piedmont in recent years and—indeed—so much of our contemporary American landscape.

THOMAS J. CAMPANELLA is a Guggenheim fellow and associate professor of urban planning at the University of North Carolina, Chapel Hill. He is the author of *The Concrete Dragon: China's Urban Revolution and What It Means for the World* and *Republic of Shade: New England and the American Elm*. He and his wife, Wu Wei, have restored two Antebellum houses in Hillsborough and one Mao-era apartment in Nanjing, China.

Dinner at the Saratoga Grill

ELON G. EIDENIER

Light brushes fresh cream
across the court house cornices,
on the portico time climbs
the clock's face. Second story

windows reflect sun. Happy
with themselves for being historic
the newly pointed bricks show
their form. This evening gloomy

clouds scurry like fugitives fleeing.
When morning comes Corinthian
columns rise to attention & grass
rolls itself out welcoming judges

as swallows circle like clerks
shuffling legal documents

ELON G. (JERRY) EIDENIER is the author of *Sonnets to Eurydice* and *Draw Fire Catch Flame*. His work has appeared in various journals, including the *Virginia Quarterly Review*, *Rhino*, *Outer Banks Magazine*, and in the anthology, *In a Fine Frenzy: Poets Respond to Shakespeare*.

Reborn Again

JOSH KASTRINSKY

THE WHITE FRAME STRUCTURE AT 219 South Nash Street is a building that has had many lives over the last century. Now it has a new life.

Bishop Zella Case is a seed-planter. Her seeds are churches, and she's planting a ministry, the Church of Promise, in that building.

She has a five-year plan. When her plan has been fulfilled, she'll move on from West Hillsborough with the intention of planting the seed elsewhere. And the Church of Promise will be here to stay.

Until then, Case is holding services for the Church of Promise and says her calling is to bring the building back to its former glory and create a mission of service from within its walls.

The Church of Promise's situation is somewhat unique, since the building she is using already has another occupant. Ida Louise Evans Lawson, who has owned the building on South Nash Street since the 1970s, began leading services for a youth ministry more than thirty years ago. More recently, she has led a ministry for the disabled, but services have been less frequent because of Lawson's health problems.

The building has not always been a house of worship. Built about 1910, it was the general store, well located for the many people employed at the mill across the street. In the 1920s, it was a hotdog stand. By the 1930s, it had become a family residence. Eventually, it became a place of worship.

Lawson was given the church in the 1970s, with a request from the former owner to keep the building's old bell ringing every Sunday.

"I want a place for [the handicapped] to practice their talent without being discriminated against," said Lawson of her ministry, which she hopes to continue operating on Saturdays, with Sundays devoted to Case's Church of Promise.

Case doesn't want to keep the small church reserved for just the two women and their individual missions; she wants to see a ministry in the building every night: "Working together [at a church] isn't something many people do," she said. "My hope is to have something happening every night.

"I believe churches should be used. If we can't work together down here, how are we ever going to get where we need to go?"

Case's ministry has roots in her western Orange County home. When she left a position with a church in Mebane and was applying to join other churches, family members requested she hold a service at home. Soon, friends began arriving.

"My 28-by-16 room started to get small," she said.

Through acquaintances, she found Lawson and the building at 219 South Nash Street.

An interior decorator by trade, Case immediately began redesigning the interior of the old building in an attempt to modernize it. The daughter of a builder, she worked alongside her husband and a family friend. She has kept the upstairs of the church—an attic space with low-hanging ceilings that speaks of an earlier era—unchanged, save for the computer at the top of the stairs, to reflect its past lives. Many aspects of the church have survived its transformations, none more visible than the narrow, steep staircase leading to the office.

When Lawson first saw the interior changes to the church, she was stunned. "The real reason I'm here is to lift her up," Case said.

For now the two women and their ministries have found a shared house of worship at 219 South Nash Street, where the bell rings every Sunday.

JOSH KASTRINSKY is a writer, and former editor and reporter for *The News of Orange County*, a weekly newspaper based in Hillsborough.

["Reborn Again" is based on an article published in the May 27, 2009, edition of *The News of Orange County*. This version appears with permission from *The News of Orange County*.]

Always

for Wesley Woods

MIKE TROY

When big or small things needed doing
For the common good,
Without asking, without fail,
Always Wesley would.

Every finite thing you need
Is at his hardware store;
It's probably been there, sitting, waiting,
Since 1944.

And in the doorway as I'd drive by,
In his plaid shirt he stood;
He'd grin and wave and call my name:
Always Wesley would.

MIKE TROY lives in West Hillsborough with his wife, fiber artist Laura Middlebrooks, and cat, Horace Williams. Mike is the town's poet laureate emeritus.

Edible Hillsborough

AARON VANDEMARK

WALKING IN EARLY JUNE, you often smell the honeysuckle before you see it. Like cut grass or lavender warmed by the sun, the afternoon honeysuckle-sweetened air is distinctly summer's musk. At the first scent, my brain starts manipulating the yellow blossoms in a mental kitchen, applying different techniques to coax out their flavor. Opportunities for culinary inspiration like this exist all over town. What follows are some of my fondest local food memories, accompanied by a dinner menu inspired by the edible parts of Hillsborough.

Purslane:
The urgency with which Ivy's sniffing lets me know she's picked up the scent of something dreadful. I tighten the leash, my eyes darting around for cat poop or road kill, two of her favorites. She's fast, but the old man's faster. I see it, jerking her leash, pulling her in another direction. I've won this round and she's none too happy about it.

We walk down Orange Street on the south side of Town Hall. She pees in the grass just off the brick sidewalk. She always stares over her shoulder at me while she's peeing, which makes me feel weird for watching her in the first place. So, I've gotten accustomed to averting my attention. I look down at the ground and see something familiar. It takes me a moment to place it, but I recognize this little weed.

It's purslane, growing heartily in the seams of the brick path. I pay for this at the farmers' market, and here it is not a block from my house, underfoot, underappreciated. I pull a pink stem with its green leaves and examine it more closely. The leaves are grouped in places along the stem like little asterisks, and I remember it tastes kind of green and sour, tender, but meaty, like young spinach. Just as I'm about to pop it in my mouth, Ivy yanks on the leash jerking my body. I drop the purslane. Son of a bitch, we're even!

Cherries, figs, pecans, chestnuts:
The generosity of my neighbors has been evident from our first days in town when Margaret Moore stoked up a conversation from her front yard. Twenty minutes later we were leaving her porch with homemade gazpacho and an invitation to "Senior Casino Night" at the Big Barn.

It's not uncommon to come home from the restaurant to find a basket of fresh figs or cherries on our door stoop with a friendly note from the Eideniers. Their cherries have made their way onto the Panciuto menu in the form of cherry cobblers with white chocolate ice cream, and their figs have been served in a salad with fried goat cheese and prosciutto.

Sometimes I find a bag of the Singers' pecans, or shelled nuts from Nancy Goodwin at Montrose, or five pounds of fresh chestnuts from Elizabeth Woodman.

These Hillsborough fruits, gifted to me by the hands that pick them, get cooked with equal affection and are consumed with appreciation by those same wonderful neighbors. It's a unique experience to be able to share.

Pumpkin:

We don't know what it is, butting up to our neighbor's picket fence, the only plant in our yard growing with any gusto in late September. We hadn't planted it. Its structure is too intentional to be a weed. The leaves are large, wonderfully green with grayish markings, and the stalks strong and many. As we are wont to do with most of our yard, we let it be, waiting for our guest to reveal its identity.

Soon enough, Ivy leads us to our answer. Wandering along the fence one morning she picks up the scent of something irresistibly edible. Her sniffing intensifies and becomes audible as her head twitches back and forth, honing in on her bounty. To her chagrin, the trail ends at our mysterious plant with apparently nothing to eat.

That's when it dawns on us. Exposed to the elements and the toll of time, last year's "porch" pumpkin had gone the way of all flesh. Rather than trash it, we figured we'd give it to the yard, and once Ivy had given up her rabid pursuit of the soupy, pulpy mess of seeds and rot, we forgot about it. Now, almost a year after we tossed that pumpkin against the fence, Ivy smells her long lost prize once again, reborn as a volunteer. As the weather cools, the plant's tendrils crawl through the grass twenty feet in each direction, accentuated by tiny green orbs.

By the end of October, these tender babies have matured into heirloom Fairytale beauties, just like their mama. Some become ornamental, while others aspire to be something more. Those with the most potential yield their intensely orange meat to the rigors of my kitchen where they are transformed into roasted, buttered, and spiced ravioli filling. Most fittingly, wrapped in pasta, they nourish the wedding party of a young lady who has grown up just three houses away. They are the most meaningful pumpkin ravioli I've ever made. From the way Ivy cleans her bowl of leftovers, she agrees.

Dandelion greens:

With my haul from the Saturday farmers' market, I pull into the gravel parking lot on Margaret Lane turning nose first into my spot, the last one on the right. In front of me is a small tuft of weeds that never gets any attention, other than to chop it back when it threatens to consume the parking lot. Tucked in with the scrabble are the most delicate little dandelion greens I've ever seen. They are a youthful green, young and tender to be sure, handfuls waiting for me.

I look around, wondering if anyone else has spied them. I have to move quickly if they are going to be mine, momentarily forgetting that most people don't get this excited about harvesting parking lot weeds. With scissors in hand, I hurry back to my prize, glad to see it remains undiscovered. With a few snips, I have as fine a green as can be found in Orange County. Lunch just got good.

Rabbits:

Set deep in the right corner of our backyard is an old hand-made shed with corrugated metal siding and a weather-beaten red tin roof. The neighbor's tree uses it as a crutch and drapes over the roof like a bad wig. Without doors, the structure sits open like a barn. The floor is a combination of dirt and old straw, caked into the mud, most broken and shorn underfoot.

We need the shed for storage space, so one morning I begin sorting the disregarded remains of someone else's life, making room for ours. I uncover rusted garden tools, seashells, cardboard scraps, and junk that wouldn't sell at a yard sale. After clearing most of it out, I turn my attention to the floor. Starting at the back corners, I rake the straw and years of debris toward the front, kicking up plumes of dust. Imagining all the cat and mouse shit and God knows what else, I try my best not to breathe.

As I get toward the front, the rake makes a *clang* sound, metal on metal. With the tines of the rake, I drag it into the grass outside. It has a turquoise patina and is the size of a diary. It's a metal sign, announcing *Bunny Crossing* and decorated with a row of bunnies.

I realize that at some point our shed had been a rabbit pen. My first thought is that a rabbit would taste good right about now. My next thought is that someone around here might still raise rabbits, and they might sell them to me for the restaurant. The setting sun doesn't give me much time to dwell on the delectable thoughts of eating rabbit. I return to clearing out the shed in the fading light, with the bunny sign safely placed on a plank shelf above the ghosts of bunnies past.

I dream about a rabbit that night. Rabbit and I are playing chess on a spring morning, discussing how he would best be prepared for dinner. He instead proposes that the winner should cook the loser. I think about this while he ponders his next move. Quite confidently, I agree. We continue talking about all manner of preparation techniques, whether it's best to roast him whole with aromatics and potatoes, or treat his separate parts with individual attention. Perhaps his magnificent legs in a delicate braise while grilling his salted haunches quickly over a hot wood fire. Either way, he says, he'd like to be served with glazed carrots. I think that's a fine idea.

It is important I know, he continues, that he is descended from domesticated stock that had since gone wild, an allusion to the flavor of his meat. Returning the favor, I thank him and inform him that I had arrived here the other way around. He thanks me kindly. Then with one fantastic and diabolical move, he says, "Check mate." I wake up.

Plums, blackberries, & peaches:
Plums are the gateway fruit.

This particular evening is one of those reprieves from the usual August heat and humidity, evoking relief of fall and motivating us to go for a walk. Aimee, Ivy, and I start out just before dusk, in the late summer light that's turning from orange to pink. Down East Union Street, a right on Cameron, then a left, into an open field off Queen Street. At the very back in the tall grass, almost hidden in the fading light, a family of deer minds their acorns. As beautiful as they are, the real prize is much closer. It's a little plum tree, just a few quiet steps into the yard, with a hundred dangling plum earrings. No one's around to see the fruit-filled branch and me reach out for each other. I have an idea whose tree this is, as the branch hands me a plum. Any guilt I feel for stealing the fruit melts away with the sugary pulp of my first bite. Juice dribbles off my bottom lip and hits the street. I toss the pit into the woods with future plums in mind.

We continue our walk, zigzagging our way through the neighborhood taking in as much of the night as possible, passing the usual suspects on unicycles, on porches, in their yards. Around the block a house, recently the home of an elderly lady sits dormant, looking sad and empty. We follow the street around the corner following the periphery of her backyard, where a big crooked tree hides the rear of her house. Behind it though is a peach tree, dressed to the nines in fuzzy peaches. I turn to Aimee, ready to make my proposal, when she flatly says, "I could steal her peaches."

I smile in shock, proud of her corruption. She slaps her hand over her mouth. "I can't believe I said that." I want to pluck a peach from the tree, but am really conflicted. This actually feels like stealing. Looking down I see a few peaches in the grass. I look to my moral compass and whisper-shout back to Aimee, "If it's on the ground, it's not stealing, right?"

She looks puzzled, unsure of the law with regard to taking fruit from the ground of dead people's yards. I pick up the best of the fallen peaches, still twice the peach you'd find in any store. It is overripe and bruised from its fall, but it is mine. Save for my conspirators, there were no living witnesses. My appetite for fruit-robbing escalates as my appetite for fruit-eating wanes. We walk on, licking peach skin from our teeth.

We make one last detour through the graveyard in the fading light, reading the tombstones, getting name ideas for our baby due in a few months. *Pymn* and *Mozelle* are fantastic, but I'm partial to *Bun*.

On the path leading back to the street there's a row of graves on one side and a bush of gorgeous blackberries on the other. Our most recent heist fresh in my mind and mouth, I am fully aware of the hundreds of deceased

A Hillsborough-Inspired Menu

Fresh figs with roasted chestnuts and honey
Poached purslane in rabbit broth
Pumpkin ravioli with pecans in butter
Fried rabbit with cherry-mustard braised dandelion greens
Plum preserves with buttermilk biscuits
Peach-blackberry cobbler with honeysuckle ice cream

people behind me. So far, I've stolen from a living and a dead neighbor, so I figure grave-robbing from a whole field of dead people is the logical next step. While Aimee walks ahead, I pinch off a handful of berries. Some are sweet as sugar, others pucker-face sour. The last one is the sweetest of the lot, and I savor it as I devise a plan to steal every piece of fruit left in town, completing my ascent from petty thief to fruit cartel Don in less than thirty minutes.

AARON VANDEMARK is the chef and owner of Panciuto in Hillsborough. The restaurant cooks with ingredients raised in our area by great farmers who keep the land, their crops, and their animals healthy and happy. Aaron and his wife, Aimee, live in Hillsborough with their son, Henry, and crazy dog, Ivy.

Views in Fiction

Hillsborough:
Where the Wild Things Are
A very short story

RANDALL KENAN

BY NOW THE SIGHT OF A DEER MADE CRAIG ROGERS SAD. At first seeing the fawns and doe about the yard had been a delight, like having Bambi roaming about your lawn, dancing, prancing, the way they would stop and watch you watching them. Their delicate lithe bodies and limber limbs. But then they started eating the baby lettuce he had hoped to grow. Baby lettuce. Mustard. Frisée. Radicchio. The deer ate it all. Every bit of it. And then, a month ago, he had hit a deer coming home late one night from Chapel Hill on Old Highway 86 . . . at first terrifying, then annoying, then inconvenient, then just sad. Damn sad. He couldn't get the image of the spent, pathetic creature out of his mind.

When he moved to Hillsborough from New Jersey, growing green things had been one of his dreams: He dreamed wild impossible dreams of wild, over-grown plants, vines, and leaves, buds in the spring, great dripping foliage in the late summer. He ordered books, catalogs, belonged to too many listservs about gardening. All his life he had been a city boy, and now, after two decades of working as a radio-oncologist, his new move to this tiny emerald town had promised a chance to finally develop his green thumb, to get in the dirt, to make acquaintance with the earth. Hello, Earth.

His brother scoffed. His brother the big city chef. His brother who was a creature of the city if ever one did exist. His brother who had not left the island of Manhattan in three years and counting. His brother who couldn't even keep a pot of rosemary alive for more than a month. "Hey, my supplier has plenty. What's the big deal?" Farmer Rogers, he would joke. "Mr. Rogers, more like it. You flit from one 'hobby' to another, Craig. Just like poetry. Whatever happened to that?"

Ouch. Older brothers are like that. ("What have you done? Your brother's blood cries out to Me from the ground!") Why bother being delicate when you can make a clean, deep cut?

Secretly he still loved poetry. That thing his sixth grade teacher had said to him never left. "Craig, you have such vivid language. Like . . . like Langston Hughes!" But he was just a poor boy, and, like his older brother, had to make sure he made good. Medical school made sure of that. But he still loved the vivid. The making of things. "Vivid" from the Latin *vivere*. To live. Sister Thomas Thérèse made sure he learned that.

So perhaps he could recapture that feeling from growing things. That possibility had been his hope. Here comes Hillsborough, a place to make it happen, to be fruitful and multiply . . . after a fashion.

He had Mayberry R.F.D. delusion, he knew. He was not a total fool. He had never been a birder, and doubted he'd ever take up that passive obsession, but he did get a thrill when he caught sight of a cardinal or a robin doing that iconic thing, plucking a worm from the ground. Norman Rockwell could have painted that. It made Craig Rogers sigh.

Unlike the owl that swooped over his car one preternaturally dark night. A classic horror story night with a storm coming up and the great hundred-year-old pecan trees swaying and rustling and groaning violently against the backdrop of ominous clouds. The thing was eagle-big, rotund. Its wingspan improbably long and wide, like some avenging angel. And the speed of the thing, through the wind. Commanding the air more than riding it. Craig Rogers was shaking when he put his key in the door that night.

Yet the bugs did take him by surprise. More than a little aback. The mosquitoes and the moths and the flies and the yellow jackets that swarmed about him one day as he tried to move a long dead tree. They attacked him like F-16s. The pain was ferocious. He screamed and hollered like a little girl. And the wee beasties drew blood! He now knew to be afraid of anything flying that was yellow.

And yes there had been squirrels aplenty in New Jersey, but these North Carolina squirrels struck him as drug-addled, sex-crazed hooligans. He asked his neighbor if there were always this many scampering about. Some years more, she said. She had put out one of those squirrel-proof bird feeders and filled it with seed. The acrobatic squirrels always got to it, like one of those high wire acts, shimmying down the line. This struck the good doctor as wrong. Early on, he began to carry a grudge against the squirrels.

The raccoons baffled him, the way they walked, the way they tried to muscle their way into the garbage cans, after midnight, like furry ninjas, the way they looked at you when you caught them, their almost-human, almost-delicate black hands, both miracle and threat.

The raccoons and the squirrels made him root for the scary owl.

Snakes? Nobody told him there would be snakes. He called the real estate agent, almost hysterical, when the black snake came and pooled up in a puddle on his front porch. The realtor's tone was that of a nurse trying to talk down a schizophrenic. "Dr. Rogers, I seriously doubt it's poisonous. It's not even copperhead season." Copperhead season?

But Craig Rogers was not one easily deterred. He enjoyed going to the new Home Depot, despite buying too many things, things he knew he would probably not use, ever. The possibilities enthralled him, the shapes of shovels, the smell of newly milled wood, the multiplicity of nails and trowels and pots and power-tillers. He had already befriended the folk who worked at the two nurseries. They knew him by name and loved to give him advice and were quick to order new varieties of whatever genus of tarragon he had read about the night before.

One fine morning: Early it was. He wanted to be on time for a meeting with a visiting specialist. Only time for one cup of coffee, but that ritual was de rigueur if his day was to work out right. He stood over the sink drinking his cup of ambition, admiring the last wisps of a disappearing fog, glad to see it was going.

It stood so still. He had heard talk, down at the hardware store on King Street, about bucks and points. Five points. What were points? he had asked. The good ole boys had chuckled at him. Of how many points this deer wore atop his majestic head, Dr. Craig Rogers was unsure. But the elaborate adornment bewitched him. The elegance of his frame. The articulate grace of the lines. The power of which his stance bespoke. The dun and speckled pelt an infinitely dense set. And though he knew it was a lie, the good doctor knew someplace inside himself that the buck was looking, across the backyard, across the Swiss chard and rocket, through the double-paned window, directly at him, into him.

So very, very still.

Though Craig was not big on photography, it occurred to him to go get his camera, to create some evidence of this presence. But it came to him that by the time he found it (probably filled with dead batteries anyway) and returned, the grand creature would be gone. It was so still.

He stood over the sink, forgetting time, and noticed, by and by, that his coffee had grown cold, and the spell slacked and he knew he must go about his day. He was surely going to be late.

He grabbed his bag and his jacket and rushed out the door. As if the promise of a premonition: The buck had vanished.

He would go about his day, trying to ungrow those growths that grew in his patients. *Metastasis*. From the Latin from the Greek. To change. To set. He would return home. He would take out pen and paper and he would try to try again.

RANDALL KENAN is the author of numerous books, including *A Visitation of Spirits*, *Let the Dead Bury Their Dead*, and, most recently, *The Fire This Time*. He is the recipient of many awards including a Guggenheim Fellowship, the Sherwood Anderson Award, and the Rome Prize from the American Academy of Arts and Letters. He is an Associate Professor of English at the University of North Carolina, Chapel Hill.

Uncle Tatlock & the Town Clock

MICHAEL MALONE

TODAY KAYE HAD AN IDEA. He was full of ideas and sometimes they drove his friend Noni crazy. "Why don't we fix the clock?" he said as they pushed their bicycles up the steep street that ended at the entrance to Noni's home. It was enormous and called Heaven's Hill. "How 'bout that?" he said. "When you run up those courthouse stairs, I'll already be up there in the steeple and we'll turn back that clock just like it happened on Insurrection Day."

Noni stopped to catch her breath. "Kaye, we can't fix that clock. That's a historic clock. My dad asked a clock expert and he couldn't fix it."

"Grandpa Tatlock can. He can fix anything." The small African American boy pushed ahead of her through the gates of Heaven's Hill.

"He can't fix history." Noni hurried to catch him. They argued but they were ten years old and still easy with one another.

So many historic markers lined Main Street in the little town of Moors, North Carolina, that visitors could not drive slowly enough to read them all. There was even a large sign beside the courthouse announcing that the

Revolutionary War had actually begun in Moors in 1772, long before Paul Revere went galloping off somewhere up North, shouting, "The British are coming! The British are coming!"

On Monday, Moors would celebrate its annual Insurrection Day, and Noni Tilden had been chosen to play the part of the brave colonial girl who had stopped the British from hanging her father on the courthouse lawn.

"Who else they gonna pick?" scoffed Kaye when he heard the news. Every summer he traveled south from Philadelphia to Moors to stay with his grandparents Tatlock and Amma King. Somebody in his grandmother's family had worked at Heaven's Hill, the large white house high above the town, ever since their ancestor Primus had been brought there as a slave almost three hundred years ago.

"Your mama's a Gordon," Kaye said, crossing his arms and nodding in his smug way. "Course, they pick you. Only part I could play is Primus the slave and he's old. I bet you're scared."

It was true that it made Noni almost sick to her stomach to think of performing in the pageant and true that she was not surprised she had been chosen to do so. Nor did it ever occur to her to defy her mother by refusing to take the part. Noni's mother was a Gordon. And everybody knew that in Moors, Gordon was the best name you could have, just as Heaven's Hill, where generations of Gordons had grown up, was the best place you could live.

Last summer Noni and Kaye had watched the Insurrection Day pageant from the roof of Moors Savings Bank. Noni's Grandfather Gordon owned the bank, and on nice days, Kaye's grandmother sat in front of it selling placemats, tea cozies, and hand towels she had embroidered with her signature sunflower logo. But this summer Noni's cousin had gone off to college. So Noni would have to take her place and play the role of Priscilla, running down the hill in a long cotton dress to try to save her Revolutionary father's life.

Insurrection Day re-enacted a day in June 1772, when a solitary young landowner, Glendower Gordon, had stormed the royal governor's residence, riding his wild white horse right up onto the terrace and into the drawing room, where he had snatched up the governor, who was seated in his favorite chair, sipping his port and reading the news from London. The port glass shattered to the floor and the news flew everywhere as Gordon galloped away with the victim.

The next morning Gordon traded the Royalist for a half dozen young farmers imprisoned in the armory, where they sat under sentence of death for gathering in the church and saying they didn't like the way the king of England was treating them. After their release, the farmers blew up the armory and fled into the woods, while Gordon bravely held off the British soldiers chasing after them.

In the fight, Gordon himself had been captured. Already known to his enemies as Proud Gordon, he so offended his captors he was given only the briefest military trial, during which he continually made "seditious and traitorous remarks." He was sentenced to hang that very day, precisely at noon by the town clock in the courthouse steeple.

The royal governor was known for his exactitude and punctuality. He had brought this great brass four-sided "pagoda" clock all the way from London and had it installed in the courthouse steeple where, on four separate faces, it told all of Moors the exact time. Whenever the governor ordered anyone in Moors to be branded or flogged or hanged, he always scheduled the event for noon precisely.

Probably the governor would have hanged Proud Gordon that noon in 1772 had it not been for Primus Gordon, one of Gordon's house slaves at Heaven's Hill. Primus had been sent that morning to the town square to take a hat of Mrs. Gordon's to the milliner. Hearing the horrible news of the fast-approaching hanging of Mr. Gordon, whom they'd all thought had gone to Edenton to visit his cousin, the slave raced home to get help.

Mrs. Gordon fainted at his report. But Proud Gordon's little daughter, Priscilla, went tearing down the dirt road from Heaven's Hill to the brick courthouse where the royal governor was just then stepping out of his coach to watch the execution. She saw her father standing on a platform under an oak bough over which a soldier was throwing a rope. Near her father, the old vicar of St. John's was begging the royal governor to be merciful. The governor, his arm broken from the way Gordon had flung him across his saddle and galloped off with him, declared there was no mercy for traitors. The crowd booed, but soldiers in red coats held them back with long steel bayonets.

Running to the top of the courthouse steps, Priscilla saw that the noose was already around her father's neck, his hands tied behind his white fluttering shirt, his pale blond hair loose from its ribbon.

"Papa!" she shouted. "Someone please save my papa!"

Upon seeing Priscilla in the crowd, Gordon called out to his daughter in words now taught in local schools and engraved on historic markers, and repeated every year on Insurrection Day: "Go home, my dear. And never forget this day. This day is not the death but the birth of freedom!"

Priscilla did not go home, or really even listen to his speech. Instead she scrambled up the narrow winding staircase to the high steeple of the courthouse where the gleaming clock sat. She was a small girl but she lifted a heavy iron rod from the floor, wedged it between two beams and the enormous swinging brass pendulum. With all her strength she held the iron in place until it stopped the pendulum with a shudder that rattled the steeple. The clock stopped. It was six minutes till noon.

As hard as she could, she twisted at the gearbox that turned the four long rods that moved the clock hands. The great iron-filigreed hands on all four clock faces slowly clicked backwards to eleven. The clock gonged eleven times so loudly that she pressed her hands to her ears. The eleven strikes rang across the square. Priscilla Gordon had made time go backwards.

Leaning out the window, she could see the crowd below on the lawn. The governor leapt out of his chair and shouted at the soldiers, the military drummer paused in his drum roll. The townspeople — confused and alarmed because the great clock never made mistakes, and because time could never go backwards unless under the spell of powerful forces —

began shoving against the red-coated soldiers, crushing them together into a tight, nervous circle.

All at once from the deep forests came a long, shrieking war cry, and through the trees thundered six young Revolutionaries flanked by a dozen Algonquians, all of them galloping together, on plow horses and mules and ponies, across the town meadow and straight toward the crowd. Behind them, dozens more men and boys, white and black, ran on foot with muskets and axes and pitchforks and sticks.

The battle between the royal troops and the Revolutionaries lasted only a few minutes. When it was over, one redcoat and two farmers were dead and the governor had fled to his coach. A few British soldiers, unable to reach their horses, clambered atop the coach or clung to the side doors, and went with him, east to safety. They never returned.

When Proud Gordon's hands were untied, he flung the noose from his neck and dashed into the courthouse. He found Priscilla up in the clock tower, exhausted, in tears, still struggling to move the gears to turn back the heavy iron hand of time. Her father brought her out to the courthouse steps. Holding her high on his shoulders, he told the crowd what she had done. And the two of them walked together back to Heaven's Hill and into history.

That was the story of Insurrection Day, acted out by the people of Moors year after year. Everything was done to perfection. The wool colonial costumes were so accurate that everyone wearing them nearly died from the heat. There was much lobbying for the best parts: Proud Gordon, the evil governor, Primus Clay, the charitable rector of St. John's, and little Priscilla. Even those who played the crowd threw themselves with earnest exuberance into their small roles.

The only problem with the pageant was the town clock. It didn't work. It hadn't worked since 1923. And after a few failed attempts by a clock expert in Raleigh to fix it, the town of Moors had given up. In 1952 when the Chamber of Commerce imagined the event called Insurrection

Day, it didn't occur to the local businessmen to bother with the old clock. In fact, they were even talking about tearing down the old courthouse itself and might have done so if their wives in the D.A.R. hadn't stopped them. To reproduce the thrilling sound of time going backwards, and so halting the execution of Proud Gordon, they substituted a recording of Big Ben to be played over a loudspeaker, a substitution that had stayed the same ever since.

"Yep, I can fix that clock," said Kaye's Grandfather Tatlock when Kaye and Noni found him asleep in his wooden wheelchair, in the shade of his favorite sycamore.

They gave him the big box of Junior Mints he'd sent them to town to buy. "Even if you could," she asked, "how can you do it in time? The pageant's tomorrow."

"Don't you doubt it," he rumbled in his low, leisurely voice. "I can fix anything. 'Cluding that clock. One of my people, name of Tall John, his mama was Algonquian, way back, he worked for the clock master that worked on that clock. Everything that clock master knew, Tall John knew. And he passed it on."

Like the Gordons, Tatlock loved to tell stories of the high deeds of ancestors, almost as much as he enjoyed lamenting missed opportunities that had robbed him of fame and fortune—for example, the credit he'd deserved for inventing Campbell's Chicken Noodle Soup, or for being the best high-school switch-hitter in the history of North Carolina baseball.

Tat was a big man in his seventies, barrel-chested and broad-backed. Many years ago he had lost his legs to diabetes, which he called the Sugar, and for which he had often threatened to sue the Veterans Hospital. Now he spent his days in his house, Clayhome, across the lawn from Heaven's Hill, watching the news of the world, which amused him, on a small brown plastic television set that, like most of his furniture, had once belonged to the owners of the larger house.

There was no denying that Uncle Tatlock had a way with broken things, a gift that people in Moors used to good advantage, bringing him everything from jammed vacuum cleaners to crippled birds. He had passed this gift to fix things on to Kaye, who loved to work beside his grandfather, helping him repair old radios and car engines. They glued shards of Indian pottery they'd found down by the nearby river. They had even wired together the bones of Tatlock's amputated legs and kept them on display in a cardboard box. Decades later, when Kaye was chief of staff of Haver University Hospital, he always said his medical ambitions had begun with Tatlock's leg bones.

Tatlock sent Kaye and Noni back down the hill to town with a big Walkie-Talkie, borrowed from a grown son who worked for a taxi company. They climbed the courthouse tower and sat on a platform in the high steeple. Kaye spoke with his grandfather on the Walkie-Talkie. Tatlock asked question after question about the clock.

That evening, the old man told the children that the clock just needed to be tinkered with by somebody who understood it. It had been out of balance "ever since that colonial girl stuck that rod in and wrenched it every which way."

"You mean me?" Noni asked. "I mean, you mean Priscilla Gordon?"

"That's right, clock's never been the same since that girl messed with it, but it had too much heart to quit for another hundred years or more. Plus it got gunked up with time and slowed down till it stopped. I feel the same way, I tell you." He sighed a great sorrowful sigh at the relentlessness of age. "But my brain and y'alls legs can take care of this business. I tell you two what to do, and you two go do it, and that clock'll be good as new by the time Noni's got to put on her show."

Kaye took away the nearly empty box of candy mints before his grandfather could eat them all. They weren't good for him. "If you could fix the clock, why didn't you?"

Tatlock shrugged, his big hands floating over his belly. "Nobody asked me."

They worked till late in the night.

The next morning was Insurrection Day. Kaye brought Tatlock down the hill in his wheelchair and stationed him right beside the hanging tree to watch the pageant. Exactly on schedule the elementary school principal, playing Proud Gordon, trotted away with the hardware store owner, playing the royal governor, on a horse borrowed from a riding stable. The Revolutionary farmers fled to the woods, and the British troops captured Gordon.

At a quarter to noon, the crowd of angry Colonists gathered at the courthouse. The royal coach (an old hansom) pulled up, and the rector of St. John's, playing the rector of St. John's, begged the governor for mercy, to no avail.

Down came Noni running from Heaven's Hill just as she had rehearsed. Even though her voice was trembling, she called out, "Papa! Someone please save my papa!" to the perfect satisfaction of her usually critical mother. But unlike at the rehearsal, Noni raced inside the courthouse and, instead of starting the recording of Big Ben, ran up the winding stairs to the steeple and into the room where her friend Kaye stood waiting. He let go of the rope that held the great heavy pendulum and set it swinging just as Noni climbed up beside him.

The great clock began to bong, ringing loudly eleven times to the complete amazement of the crowd below. The iron-filigreed hands on all four clock faces moved precisely, together, minute by minute, telling time. The crowd stared and then they clapped and shouted.

No one knew who had fixed the clock. No one suspected the two children or the old African American man in the wheelchair who quietly watched from the audience. Some believed the town secretly had hired an expert from a big city. Some believed it was the ghost of Priscilla Gordon. And in a way it was.

As the townspeople stood debating who was responsible, Tatlock yelled to Kaye and Noni, "Push me on home, children. Push fast as you can."

"You'll fall!" Noni worried.

"Honey, listen to me, you gotta go all out going down, or you never gonna make it going all the way up! That's true of this hill and that's true of this life."

So Kaye and Noni ran behind the wheelchair, shoving it as hard as they could, until the hill steepened and the chair was racing so fast downward that they couldn't keep up as it zigzagged wildly in the middle of the street, terrifying Noni that it was going to topple over and kill the old man.

But Tatlock flew without mishap to the bottom of the hill and then, his hands pumping the wheels, he climbed the other side, slowing on the incline so that Noni and Kaye reached him half way up the street. The two children pushed the chair over the crest and in through the iron gates that guarded Heaven's Hill.

From there the three conspirators looked back down at the courthouse where Amma Clay King, Kaye's grandmother and Tatlock's wife, was selling the last of her souvenirs to the last of the tourists. They heard the clock strike twelve. Time was going on again in Moors.

"I'll tell you another day that clock rang out special," Tatlock said, waiting for Noni and Kaye to catch their breath before pushing him up the gravel drive to his house. "Eighteen-sixty-five. My great-grandpa was a boy right here down the road that day, and he heard that clock chiming when the time come for the generals to walk out of that little house over there. . . ." Tatlock pointed at a small frame house near the courthouse.

"What generals?" asked Kaye.

"Confederate. They had to give it up, right here in Moors. Surrender to the Yankees. Twelve o'clock noon, out they came, all dressed up and stiff-faced. That clock in the courthouse rang the hours. My great-granddaddy heard it ring, and he said how it was like a bell in his heart, how that clock was ringing out freedom that day. The end of the war, and it was a happy day for all our people. Not that things got much better."

123

". . . Why didn't you ever leave here, Grandpa?" Kaye frowned. "You're still right here in Moors and so is Grandma Amma. And just about everybody you know. Why you wanna stay here?"

Tatlock scratched at his large gun-black cheek as he looked out over the green hills of Moors and at the rose gold sky brightening the steeple spire above the town. "It's my home," he said. "Just like it's hers." He took Noni's small hand in his. "It's our home. And time changes things. You just have to wait."

Noni smiled. "If you can fix time."

"I guess he can," grinned Kaye.

Noni and Kaye pushed Grandpa Tat back to Clayhome. And after supper they sat with him, watching Insurrection Day on the local news, and the news of the world outside the world they knew.

MICHAEL MALONE has written over a dozen books, including *Handling Sin*, *Time's Witness*, *Uncivil Seasons*, and *Four Corners of the Sky*. A former television writer, Michael is the recipient of numerous awards, including the Emmy, O Henry, and Edgar. He is a professor of theater studies at Duke University.

Scenes from *On Agate Hill*

LEE SMITH

FRANKLY — HAVING GROWN UP IN THE APPALACHIAN SOUTH — I never gave much of a damn about the Civil War. But then my husband and I moved into an old house smack in the middle of Hillsborough, and it was like walking into history. I found myself musing over those heartbreakingly short dates and "C.S.A." carved into many of the mossy tombstones in the Presbyterian Church cemetery right next door.

Down on the corner, the Orange County Historical Museum holds a fine collection of Civil War artifacts, everything from rifles to photographs — all those uniformed boys staring out solemnly into the unimaginable future. I couldn't quit looking at them. Best of all was the museum's curator Dr. Ernest Dollar, a recent PhD from the Southern Studies program down in Chapel Hill, a young man on fire with history. He deluged me with Civil War letters, books, and diaries, including a diary kept by a young girl at the Burwell School, one block away, where the admirable Anna Burwell had started her academy for young women in 1837.

I walked up Churton Street to visit the school. Mrs. Burwell turned out to be a novelist's dream. She had stood six feet tall, robustly built, pious, and well read. She had twelve children and could recite *Paradise Lost* by heart.

Suddenly I realized that I was going to write a novel about a young girl orphaned by the Civil War, and that she would attend a school such as the Burwell School, and . . . I was off and running.

—Lee Smith
Hillsborough
November 2009

Some Hillsborough-Inspired Scenes from On Agate Hill

A SELECTION FROM THE DIARY OF MOLLY PETREE

November 19, 1872

Dear Diary,

Now we have been to the Tableaux Vivants, the best and most beautiful thing I have ever witnessed though I did not want to go at first as Aunt Cecelia said they are edifying. Well she has edified me almost to death all ready but Mary White said, Oh do come, Molly, you will love it, you can wear my blue velvet dress! So we took the carriage with Virgil driving and even he was dressed up. Where did you get that hat? I asked him. . . .

Thus we arrived in front of the square two-story Masonic Lodge which was all lit up, every window blazing, luminaries placed at intervals from the road to the steps of the hall. Oh, look! cried Mary White. For we were greeted at the door by a personage in a turban and a shimmering gold cloth wrap, whether man or woman I could not say. Kerosene lamps lined the wooden stage, and other huge lanterns hung on ropes, as dazzling as the sun. Beautiful music came down from the balcony where only a few candles glowed, so as not to take away from the tableaux. Every chair in town must have been gathered up for the audience, while we children sat on the floor at the front. Adeline and Ida complained.

Laydees and gentlemen! The velvet curtain parted and out came Doctor Lambeth dressed in a top hat and tails. Everyone cheered. The ladys of the Hillsborough Relief Association welcome you to their Tableaux. You may rest assured that all proceeds from this event will go toward the care of the neediest among us, especially widows and orphans of the Confederacy. <u>And now, on with the show!</u> Doctor Lambeth bowed low to the crowd which screamed when two birds flew out of his upraised hat and swooped around the hall, finally to disappear in the vast dark shadowy balcony where the hidden musicians were playing dramatic music.

And now—Doctor Lambeths gray hair streamed down to his shoulders—And now, allow me to take you back in time to ancient Greece where we shall present The Nine Muses!

Two little boys dressed in red suits appeared at the center of the stage then went running back on each side to pull the heavy curtains open revealing a classical scene like an engraving from a mythology book. Everyone in the audience gasped. Applause began and continued. The Muses did not respond to the cheers but held their poses perfectly, moving not a muscle. They looked like statues. White columns of varying heights stood at either side of this tableau, while the floor in front of the Muses was strewn with cunning cloth roses. Aunt Cecelia had edified us so much we all ready knew that the Muses were nine in number, daughters of Jupiter and the Goddess of Memory, Mnemosyne. We all ready knew their names too which were written out on placards in fancy printing.

Each white-gowned Muse had a placard propped up in front of her. Calliope, Muse of Epic Poetry and Rhetoric, wore a Grecian war helmet over her long golden curls. One pretty hand rested on the short sword stuck in the rope at her waist, while she glared off to the side at some oncoming enemy army. Red spots gleamed on her cheeks. But the one I most wanted to be was Tragedy, who knelt in an attitude of misery and dispair. Her head was bowed so low that we could not even see her features. She wore a crown of myrtle leaves over her smooth black hair.

Polyhymnia, the Muse of Religious Hymns, held a songbook aloft and appeared to be singing vigorously. This meant that she had to stand still with her mouth wide open which is very hard, Mary White and I have since tried it. Plain red-headed Clio sat at a little spindly-legged writing desk wearing gold-rimmed spectacles, looking down at a huge thick book which said HISTORY across its cover. Erato, the prettiest, held one hand to her heart for she was the Muse of Love Songs.

The Muse of Lyric Poetry, Euterpe, appeared to be begging someone for something, arms outstretched, her face in anguish. The great fat girl who wore a jesters hat was Thalia, the Muse of Comedy. She looked like a big puffy cloud in her billowing dress. I poked Mary White and pointed, for Thalia was the best, really. You had to laugh when you looked at her. Urania was a serious round-faced girl who carried the moon in one hand and a little globe of the earth in the other. She is the Muse of Astronomy. Terpischore wore full white trousers and held a difficult dance pose, to everyones amazement. Immediately I wanted to be her, instead of Tragedy.

Everyone in the hall clapped, some crying out, <u>Bravo, bravo!</u> But the Muses did not move, or acknowledge the applause in any way, holding their attitudes. We all jumped to our feet, still clapping. Some wags called out things such as <u>Watch out there Lucinda, you are going to drop the moon!</u> Or <u>why so sad Betsy?</u> while others said, <u>Hush boys, hush!</u> We were directly in front of Tragedy who looked up once and gave us a wink. The curtain was drawn back together by the two little boys who opened it, one of them stumbling over his own feet to the crowds delight. <u>Bravo,</u> they called out to him.

I just do not think a married woman should participate in something like this. It is not right! Aunt Cecelia said severely to the widow Brown while a lot of bumping and scraping went on behind the curtain as the association prepared for the next Tableau, advertised as <u>The Death Scene from Romeo and Juliet.</u> Mary White and I could not wait for this one, as we had read the entire play in preparation, and it promised to be even more tragic than Tragedy. There was scattered applause here and there as the Muses came out to join the audience.

Then the descending hush, then Doctor Lambeth bowed low and announced, <u>Romeo and Juliet, the Death Scene,</u> in a deep and serious tone. The fiddle wailed down from the balcony. Mary White and I held hands. This time, Calliope and Urania opened the curtain. We had to crane our necks to see, for a lot of this scene took place on the floor.

Now the columns supported an arch, the entrance to the Capulet tomb. Flares burned in sconces. There lay Romeo dead on his back, the vial of poison still in his hand. Fair Juliet, also dead, lay in a pool of crimson created by the skirt of her silk dress. The jeweled hilt of the dagger jutted up from her chest, catching the torch light—later, Mary White and I figured out that she had thrust it under her armpit. But it looked perfectly real, exactly like she had stabbed herself. Another young man lay dead beside her.

That must be Paris, Mary White whispered pointing at this body whose sword lay at his side.

Or maybe Tybalt? I couldnt remember.

Friar Lawrence, whose face was hid in the hood of his gown, a plain old rope tied around his waist, stood leaning on a twisted cane. A soldier in uniform stood outside the tomb, arms crossed, while a King and Queen in gold crowns knelt by the bodies. Dazzling sparks of light glinted off the crowns, the swords, the jewels. Sad music from the balcony floated down over all. This time, no applause, but a general intake of breath, a huge gasp. Sobs were heard around the room.

Then I caught on.

Though Romeo wore a cap, a blue silk vest, black tights, and fancy pantaloons tucked into his high black boots, clearly he was a girl, one of the members of the Hillsborough Relief Association, her features calm and classical in death, large nose, dark brow. Paris too was a girl, as was the Watchman, the King, and even Friar Lawrence!

Why, Romeo is one of those Walker girls! The widow Brown exclaimed aloud, causing titters throughout the hall.

The mood was broken. Excited conversation erupted everywhere, as the Muses raced across the stage dragging the heavy curtain shut.

Doctor Lambeth came back out. Laydees and gentlemen, it has been our great pleasure —, he began, but his voice was lost in the hubbub.

Who was responsible for the choice of this scene? A pig-faced man demanded angrily, while another man said that personally he found Romeo and Juliet to be totally charming and elevating in the manner of all great tragedy.

Oh poppycock! A skinny lady with spectacles said to our right.

Adeline! Ida! shrilled the widow.

Stay right where you are, Aunt Cecelia said severely, pointing to us. She did not look a bit edified. She held her special-smelling handkerchief to her face while we waited for the widow to grab up Adeline and Ida. Then Aunt Cecelia set forth across the hall, followed by the widow Brown. Mary White and I came in their wake, straight out the big double doors into the dark chilly night. I had to hold up the skirt of the blue velvet dress, which was too long for me, as off we went down the street toward the widows house.

Well! Aunt Cecelia said. I must say I had misunderstood the nature of this spectacle. The Muses were all well and good, but Romeo and Juliet went beyond the pale, dont you agree, Muriel? And good heavens, those costumes — girls in pants, in public! What has become of modesty? of femininity? I would like to know. Young ladys should not appear in public at all if their judgment is shown to be this faulty, this rash. Especially not young married ladys, the very idea.

Oh come now, Sissy, the widow Brown said in her high voice. Certainly there can be no immodesty in a young lady doing something which the whole community approves. Why these Tableaux are performed everywhere now, they are quite the thing. And look at how much money they must have raised, and for a very good cause, I might add.

<u>To say that a thing is done does not make it right, Muriel.</u> Each of Aunt Cecelias words came out in a puff of white breath as we paused by the last streetlight on our way back.

You need not preach to me, my dear. The widow sounded mad. Perhaps you have been too long in the country.

Country has nothing to do with it, I assure you, Aunt Cecelia said. Those girls were not comporting themselves as ladys. Mark my words, this never would have happened before the War.

Then it is high time for a few changes, the widow said. No one thought I could take over for Alfred either and yet I have done so quite competently if I do say so myself. For the widow owns and operates the Brown Printing and Engraving Co. Inc.

<u>It is a completely different issue.</u> Aunt Cecelia bit off each word.

No, I dont think it is, the widow said, but then we were there and all the dogs ran out barking. The carriage stood in front of the widows house with Virgil ready to tuck us all under the robes. Then he clicked to the horses and off we went through the clean and starry night.

<u>Molly?</u> It was Mary White coming forward to sit on the bench with me and Virgil. Isnt it beautiful? Mary White said, and I said, Yes. It is beautiful. Soon she was asleep too, her head against my shoulder, her breathing as light as little Junius. Aunt Cecelia snored in the back. I made sure that Mary White was fully covered by the robes. As for me, I was much too excited to sleep. The dew fell all around us, turning fast to frost which had given the whole countryside a shine well before we reached Agate Hill. I pushed the robe down so I could feel the frost on my face, for I want to feel everything Dear Diary. I want to feel everything there is. I do not want to be a lady. Instead I want to be in a Tableaux Vivant myself, I want to be Tragedy, I want to be Juliet, I want to be Romeo. <u>Thus with a kiss I die.</u>

SELECTIONS FROM THE JOURNAL OF

MARIAH RUTHERFORD SNOW

† † †
# For No One's Eyes

July 20, 1873

My attempt having ended in terrible Argument, I excused myself from the breakfast table & went out to water the plants on the porch. Not five minutes had passed before I sensed the silent presence of Dr. Snow behind me. I continued my work, every nerve on edge. "What is it?" I finally whirled about to ask, whereupon he told me frankly that Simon Black is paying so much money to Gatewood Academy that we shall be able to meet our note after all, plus send our own boys off to their respective Boarding Schools as planned, AND have adequate funds left over for repairs to the Academy!

"So you see we have no Choice," he said, following me along the row of pots. "Simon Black has made a substantial investment in this Academy."

"But Dr. Snow, that is Bribery!" I said, though I dared not turn to see his face.

"On the contrary, Mariah, it is Business. Do I make myself clear?" He gripped my elbow so tightly that I cried out in pain, dropping my bucket which rolled off the porch spilling water. "Furthermore, I consider it our Christian duty to save this girl. And frankly I am surprised that you, of all people, do not see it this way, Mariah, given your own circumstances." (He WOULD have to bring this up, of course!) "Nothing happens without God's Knowledge; remember that, Mariah. Molly Petree has been sent to us for a reason. The Lord works in mysterious ways, & it is not up to us to question Him. I know you will do your best with her."

"Dr. Snow," I said, "you are hurting my arm."

But he did not release it, pulling me toward him & into the house where to my surprise he exercised his Conjugal Rights upon the hall bench in broad daylight. He seems to be quite worked up, in general, by all that has transpired. I occupied myself by reciting the beginning of Paradise Lost all the while, finishing about the same time he did.

Today I took my cold bath a bit earlier than usual.

Of course Dr. Snow is right, & I am wrong, & ungrateful & evil & low-minded, imagining only the worst for reasons he understands all too well. Yet I shall endeavor to rise above myself, & be worthy of Simon Black's trust, & live up to Dr. Snow's opinion of my capabilities, & understand that in all matters of Business, he knows best. (Yet WHY does he know best? Oh stop it, Mariah.) Better I should remember the words of John Milton:

> The mind is its own place, and in itself
> Can make a Heaven of Hell, a Hell of Heaven.

Yet I confess I do not like her, this girl, this Molly Petree. I can not like her, pure & simple, though she looks presentable enough now, bathed & clothed, albeit Sullen & Quiet as ever. There is something about her I do not trust, some dormant spirit I sense within her — though she looks so meek & mild, I have the distinct feeling that she could do anything. Anything.

And there is something else I must confess as well. When I have closed my eyes to Pray these past two nights, I have seen — unaccountably — His face. I mean Mr. Simon Black's face: that heavy brow, those steady dark eyes looking into mine when he said, "I trust you implicitly, Mrs. Snow." Oh why is this new Trial visited upon me? And who is this Mrs. Snow? I sometimes ask myself. And who are all these Children, Mrs. Snow's Children? Eight of them! & another on the way. I am locked in a golden chest, I am bound round & round by a silken rope. Simon Black should not trust me. Nobody should trust me! For I am filled with the most base & contradictory impulses, no matter how I struggle to be worthy of God's love, & do His bidding in this world, & live up to my Responsibilities.

Mariah Rutherford Snow
Headmistress, Gatewood Academy
Hopewell, Virginia

† † †
For No One's Eyes

February 9, 1874

Today I attended to the Housekeeping as usual, went in school & heard three classes, but by the time the Pork came, I changed my dress, went out & with my own hands trimmed seventy-four pieces of meat, then came in, washed & dressed up in my best & walked up the Cedar Walk to call upon Mrs. Joseph Devereaux in the Village, Miss Pleasants that was. Then I went to Dr. Barney's, to Dr. Greene's, to Mr. Vogelsong's Pharmacy, & thence home, thank goodness at least Dr. Greene is sympathetic to a lady's Plight, for a lady must finally sleep, must she not? Rather than lying awake with awful thoughts in her head that even her old friend John Milton cannot keep at bay.

I presided at supper & the day was finished with a lecture on Eastern Religions by Professor Theodore Grumly retired from the University of Virginia, during which some of our girls Dozed Off, unfortunately. I have made a list, I shall speak to them. I am rethinking my rule of not allowing them to do handwork during lectures, at least it might keep them awake.

And in the end they shall all have more to do with mending & tatting than with Philosophy. I noticed Molly Petree listening quite intently, however; who knows what she is thinking, the little Heathen.

Mariah Rutherford Snow
Headmistress, Gatewood Academy
Hopewell, Virginia

---

† † †
For No One's Eyes

April 25, 1874

Gave birth.

Mariah Rutherford Snow
Headmistress, Gatewood Academy
Hopewell, Virginia

---

† † †
For No One's Eyes

April 27, 1874

Dear Lord, I shall try to love this Child as I try to love all my Children, yet I confess my Sorrow at having a girl, for I know how she will struggle in this world. The burdens of our sex are heavy. Yet I believe I will name her Susannah in hopes that she will have a happier Spirit & Lighter Heart than her mother.

Mariah Rutherford Snow
Headmistress, Gatewood Academy
Hopewell, Virginia

†††
For No One's Eyes

May 3, 1874

At last Dr. Snow has come in to see the child, he has named her Frances Theodosia, for his Mother, whom I Hated with all my being. Yet I suppose it does not matter, after all. For what's in a name? as the Bard asks. We lose our names as we lose our Youth, our Beauty, & our Lives.

Mariah Rutherford Snow
Headmistress, Gatewood Academy
Hopewell, Virginia

137

LEE SMITH is the author of twelve novels, including *Fair and Tender Ladies* and *The Last Girls*, and four collections of short stories, most recently, *Mrs. Darcy and the Blue-Eyed Stranger*. She is the recipient of an Academy Award in Fiction from the American Academy of Arts and Letters. *On Agate Hill* was published in 2006 by Algonquin Books and received the Thomas Wolfe Memorial Literary Award.

In the Country 🍀

The Cedars of Lebanon

HAL CROWTHER

Annihilating all that's made/To a green thought in a green shade.
—Andrew Marvell, "The Garden"

THE CITY FATHERS OF OXFORD, MISSISSIPPI, voted to celebrate William Faulkner's 100th birthday by commissioning a monument to Oxford's most famous native son. To clear a place in the courthouse square the novelist immortalized, they set their chainsaws to an old magnolia tree.

Faulkner was known to have a great affection for trees, hardly any for statues. (Remember Benjy's voice in *The Sound and the Fury*: "Caddy smelled like trees . . . Caddy smelled like trees in the rain.") His family responded with outrage.

"I'm horrified about the magnolia tree and the statue," Faulkner's daughter, Jill Summers, told the aldermen. "Please honor my father's often repeated wish for privacy. I do not want the statue of my father put on the square or anywhere else."

Misunderstanding, mortification, impasse. So it has always been and always will be, when politicians try to pay their respects to art. But the magnolia that knew William Faulkner lies dismembered in a landfill, and in our lifetime nothing—granite, bronze, or vegetable—will replace the shade or the dignity it supplied.

Trees have been much on my mind. The big machines have come to Hillsborough's old town cemetery, just beyond my garden fence, to clear the trees uprooted by a hurricane named Fran. The storm toppled nearly everything except a mammoth magnolia. A few months later the wretched village elders, citing their fear of another hurricane, sneaked into the cemetery at dawn and cut down that venerable magnolia, too.

For months two great trunks lay across a shattered stone wall, their roots gripping pieces of headstones and vaults, and dark fragments of wood that could have been ancient coffins. We looked away and looked back again, with morbid curiosity, anticipating something more alarming poking out of those red root-clots of clay.

A signer of the Declaration of Independence still rests just over the wall, along with an antebellum governor and a long roster of dignitaries buried here since the eighteenth century. But the cemetery isn't the place it was last summer, or for two hundred summers before that, when you could read the epitaphs or sit and read your book in the deepest, coolest, most poetic shade the township could provide. Direct sunlight looks rude and garish on mossy headstones that haven't felt the sun since Jeff Davis was president.

Maybe it's only our graves—after a century or two—that manage a dignity of their own. Stripped of trees, most of the real estate we trade and covet, most of the habitations of the human race look as dignified as Robert Dole in running shorts.

It was the most terrible year for the trees. A hurricane takes only an hour to accomplish a devastation that armies of savage developers couldn't manage in a decade. Raleigh, the City of Oaks, was altered forever by Fran, as Charleston was altered by Hugo. (Excuse Southern paranoia, but if it had been a northern state capital, like Boston or Harrisburg, the city's tragedy would have led every network newscast. To the New York media, hurricanes in the Carolinas are as remote and generic as typhoons in Bangladesh.)

I didn't dare to ask whether the storm spared the Rose Garden, once my tree-rich sanctuary in the heart of Raleigh. But the hurricane's most catastrophic effects were out in the woods, far from the towns and traffic. The damage to my own property—two dozen trees destroyed or permanently disfigured—represented a small fraction of what this devil storm has cost me.

For years before I owned a house and trees, I rented them—in Wake, Durham, Orange, and Chatham counties. I rented some green and decent places, though my lot in North Raleigh was surrounded by bulldozers creating new subdivisions, and a pine grove in Durham where I read novels in perfect solitude is now the parking lot of the Sheraton. But mostly I appropriated places in parks and in the public forests, which usually belong to our universities. I always saw myself as a connoisseur of green places where a daydreamer could hide.

I can't explain why the loneliest places draw the wrath of the storm. Do buildings themselves act as windbreaks, so that a domino effect occurs when the hurricane roars through a forest far from human habitations? Go see my favorite places for yourself. At UNC's Mason Farm in Chapel Hill, half of the old oak forest that inspired naturalist John K. Terres was lying in the swamp, or in chain-sawed segments along the trail.

East of campus, in the North Carolina Botanical Garden, it was far worse. Hundreds of huge trees were stretched out in neat rows, like wheat straw behind a thresher. There's a place near the top of the hill, once forest, where no tree thicker than your wrist was still standing, for two hundred yards. In another place, a natural bowl, one of Fran's tornadoes uprooted every tree like a giant eggbeater.

The Duke Forest off Whitfield Road was a grim boneyard of fallen trees, and the scenic meanders of New Hope Creek were still choked with the storm's debris. In the elbow bend of the Eno River west of Hillsborough, my favorite grove of all, with twenty years of memories, was reduced to a natural clear-cut. The Eno, humiliated, flowed sluggishly through a hopeless rubble of logs. When we walked the trail months later, even my dog seemed depressed.

They were my places. There are several I won't visit anymore. To me that feels very much like the death of a friend, or saying good-bye to one you don't expect to see again.

Trees fall, cities spread. Rising generations, and future ones, will adjust to what they have, find shade where they can. Natural selection favors individuals who sleepwalk through whole seasons in city apartments, who would rather shop or Netsurf than walk three blocks to the park; who can live anywhere without really noticing, and never seek green sanctuary.

Spawned by nomadic company families, raised in subdivisions, they increasingly outnumber those of us from small towns, those of us from mountains who resonate to the prose of Edward Abbey (author, tree-spiker, anarchist, onetime teacher at Western Carolina in Cullowhee) in *Appalachian Wilderness*:

> The trees. Vegetation cradle of North America. All those trees transpiring patiently through the wet and exhilarating winds of spring, through the heavy, sultry, sullen summers into the smoky autumns. Through the seasons, years, millennia. . . . The hill country in North Carolina, eastern Kentucky and Tennessee seems today something like Punxsutawney, Pa., 50 years ago, or Home, Pa., where we grew up. All of it Appalachian, winter or summer, then or now. Land of the breathing trees, the big woods, the rainy forests.

(True, Abbey migrated to the desert Southwest. But he earned his living as a fire lookout in the national forests.)

We'll soon be anachronisms, subjects like me who discover at a midway point in our lives that it was always trees, not houses, that constituted home. Anyone with enough money can have his house any way he chooses, even the way it looked in 1797. But trees are a legacy, subject to cancellation without notice, maintained with luck, love, faith, and vigilance. Some of the most fundamental grooves in our consciousness are formed by the way familiar trees divide, disperse, and define the daylight in which we live.

Think of coming home, after fifty years, to the place where you were raised. If all the trees are in place, you can imagine a vanished house more than adequately; if all the trees are gone, the house in its nakedness is just a pile of bricks and kindling. I'm unsentimental about the house where I grew up, because almost all my trees have vanished—some condemned for such trivial sins as attracting squirrels. I recoil when I drive by my grandfather's house, sold out of the family forty years ago, where unspeakable barbarians cut down his whole orchard and his vineyards as well, replacing them with a single swing set on three acres now flat and featureless as a billiard table.

Call my condition arboreal dependency. In his brilliant book, *Landscape and Memory*, Simon Schama argues that the psyches of great nations—among them England, Germany, and the United States—were formed in the forest primeval. England's morale has never fully recovered, he suggests, from the Great Storm of 1703 that uprooted 7,000 oaks in the New Forest and the Forest of Dean.

I believe it. In my front yard there was a seventy-foot hickory tree the storm blew halfway over, before a maple broke its fall. It was the best tree in my new yard. At irresponsible expense I hired some young men with a tow truck to crank it nearly vertical, rebury its roots, and cable it in place.

The effect was not *Better Homes and Gardens*—five thick cables held it and the tree still leaned to the southeast at around eighty degrees. Some neighbors called my disabled veteran "Crowther's Folly." Tourists pointed. But one spring day there were new leaves on that hickory, and it was the finest I thing I had to celebrate all year.

HAL CROWTHER is a Mencken Award–winning essayist and critic. A former newsmagazine editor, screenwriter, and syndicated columnist, he is the author of *Gather at the River*, *Cathedrals of Kudzu*, *Unarmed But Dangerous*, and the upcoming *Departures*. His wife is the novelist Lee Smith.

You Can Walk the Eno

ELON G. EIDENIER

as it snakes
between farm & home
on its banks no longer
the Occoneechee can be found,
the smudge of fire has disappeared,
the black of hair, the high cheek bones.

Not so long ago this land was theirs,
berries & roots, fish & bird.
They curved bows from the Osage
Orange & hunted deer at the river.

What did the young girl think
when she reached for tokens
from strangers & offered
a basket of fish in return,
no way to know how sickness
would end a world?

At the dig I look, the newly
opened grave shows her bones
the outline of body. She still
wears a necklace of shells.

ELON G. (JERRY) EIDENIER is the author of *Sonnets to Eurydice* and *Draw Fire Catch Flame*. His work has appeared in various journals including the *Virginia Quarterly Review, Rhino, Outer Banks Magazine,* and in the anthology, *In a Fine Frenzy: Poets Respond to Shakespeare.*

A Gardener's Journal

NANCY GOODWIN

A Day in the Garden: Monday, June 23

THE DAY BEGINS WITH THE LIGHT. I open one eye to see whether the sun is high enough to let me know, without glancing at the clock, whether to get up. While Craufurd makes coffee and squeezes fresh orange juice, I walk slowly down to the gates to pick up the paper. On this morning I go through the Circle Garden to see whether seeds are ripe on the burgundy poppies and the pink-flowered *Paeonia broteroi* that bloomed in April.

After breakfast I walk the new fence line with Angie, our Australian shepherd/Border collie mix, to see whether a limb has fallen on the fence or a deer has crashed through it. The walk is slow and deliberate as I feel the fence for tears and pause to look for motion from deer inside or outside the protection we have just installed. Recently the fence was broken down in two places, so I know I have at least one adult deer on the wrong side — the garden side.

I open the doors on the big greenhouse and water the cuttings in their pots on the propagation mat. I welcome Anne Cousineau who has come to help with the garden. She mulches part of the Tropical Garden and north of the fence where tiny rooted gardenias struggle for survival. I return to yesterday's task, which is to dig up the sod between the pump house and the garden surrounding the law office, one of several nineteenth-century outbuildings at Montrose. I dig the soil six to eight inches deep and delight in the wrenching sound of the roots coming up. Then I turn over the clumps so that the earth is on top with grass roots up and old blades of grass on the bottom. It is slow work. I am creating a new path where grass used to grow and where Craufurd can no longer mow. Anne and I mulch the area heavily.

Following that, we pull out the old poppies. Seeds we have collected during the past few weeks we now separate according to color and store for fall sowing. We edge the border, cut back the dahlias, and imagine how it will look tomorrow after we plant it with tropical plants.

After lunch, Anne waters the nursery stock and I return to weed an unfinished section of the garden north of the fence. This area is where we will dig in tender plants including phormiums and alpinias still in their pots. I work beneath the metasequoia I grew from a seed sown shortly after we moved to Montrose [in the late 1970s]. A pesky bamboo, escaped from a pot left near the fence fifteen years ago, and *Vinca major* has spread throughout the area.

I make great progress and am beside the fence when I see a copperhead slowly slithering through the plants I am weeding. Anne watches where the snake goes while I go for help. The snake never reappears. With the vision of the snake in mind, I cut the green foliage with shears before digging out the remaining weeds. I sweep the area with a long iron rod, but the snake has vanished.

A group of local men comes to cut and take away a hackberry tree that has fallen to a 45-degree angle over the driveway. It takes a cherry picker, two big dump trucks, one pick-up truck, and six men to cut and clear the debris from the tree.

This gives me my opportunity to release the deer from the confines of the garden. I walk slowly down the path to the west side of the pond.

As I approach the fence, I notice a doe slowly walking next to the fence. I stop and stand as still as possible. The doe takes a while to see me, but when she finally does, she snorts and runs back toward St. Mary's Road. I open the gate and then circle back about a hundred feet toward the house and away from the fence.

Again I walk toward the fence but about a hundred feet farther north than before. Just as I am almost in sight of the pond, I see the deer near the fence and going south. I believe she runs through the gate, for I never see her again. I close the gate and walk slowly through the woods.

As I turn the corner to go west I see two large birds with red crests and realize that they are a pair of pileated woodpeckers. Each pecks at the trunk of a tree and they chatter away at each other. Both fly to a nearby tree where they continue pecking and chattering, and there I leave them.

It is a full day and a pleasantly exhausting one. Tomorrow will be different although the setting will be similar, and I will plant in the beds prepared today and clear the May Garden for its summer plantings. I go to bed full of optimism for the gardens I will plant and full of hope for continued rain throughout the summer. It is a day never to be repeated and yet much will be similar tomorrow. There is diversity in repetition.

Another Day in the Garden: Tuesday, June 24

The beginning of this day is a little different from most. Craufurd and I walk next door to Cameron Park School to vote in two run-off elections. I begin my walk around the protected parts of the garden later than usual but I see no deer.

Today two people help me: Anne Cousineau, who has been working here for about seven months, and Cathy Dykes, who has worked with me for more than seven years. Both of these gardeners are capable, hard-working, cheerful people with whom I love to plan, plant, and maintain the garden.

Anne collects poppy seeds, carefully organizing them by color, while Cathy and I go to the nursery to select plants for the garden on the south side of the law office. This part of the garden is important for it is at the entrance to the main sunny gardens and precedes the Tropical Garden. The plantings have to establish the spirit of the gardens to follow. Just a month ago, this garden contained one of our major poppy displays.

For our summer planting we choose tibouchinas, punicas (pomegranates), Red Shield hibiscus, bright chartreuse-leaved durantas, a large potted *Euphorbia cotinifolia*, *Homalocladium platycladum*, *Colocasia* 'Black Magic', *Setaria palmifolia*, *Pennisetum setaceum* 'Rubrum', *Lantana* 'Radiation', red-flowered pentas, and a tall red-leaved cordyline. We place the plants in their pots, stand back, discuss the problems and move them around. We even plant some of the plants and then, after study and discussion, dig and move them. We fertilize everything with Plant-tone or Flower-tone depending on whether the plant was selected for foliage or flowers. After nearly five hours of planning and planting, I water the plants in while Cathy selects more plants for other sections of the gardens. Anne waters the nursery stock. I water all of the plants in pots along the boxwood border and throughout the sunny gardens. I pick up the empty pots, sort, and store them with their types on the slope of gravel at the edge of the woods.

Anne and Cathy leave at about 4:00, and I take another walk toward the pond looking for deer. I am elated to find no sign of any visitors. As I walk through the woods looking for ripe peony seeds, I see an enormous barred owl fly silently across the path. The seeds are nearly ready and I don't want to miss a single one so I will look every day until I've gathered all of them.

The men return in late afternoon and finish cutting down the hackberry and dead juniper. They cut the dead top out of the *Magnolia macrophylla* I had brought with me when we moved to Montrose thirty-one years ago. The magnolia is listed as "cottonwood tree" on their bill. I believe our woodsmen have never before seen a deciduous magnolia.

I come in early to prepare supper in time for Craufurd to get to a meeting in Chapel Hill by 7:00. Although it has been a short day—only eight hours—I believe the garden looks better tonight than it did this morning.

A Day Alone: Sunday, June 29

The day begins for me later than usual. I take a walk around the perimeter of the protected area at a slower pace than usual and find the fence intact and no signs of deer. When I return to the garden, I bring over my cart loaded with tools. I take another cart to the nursery to collect plants—basil, *Helianthus angustifolius* 'Lemon Queen', a new *Salvia microphylla*, and six young seedlings of *Ricinus zanzibariensis*. I go to the basement and bring up trays of dry *Tigridia pavonia* corms in their original seed flat, *Gladiolus callianthus* 'Murielae', and large bulbs of *Hymenocallis festalis* (Peruvian daffodil). I take a third cart with four buckets to the compost pile where I fill them with black, moist compost. Before leaving, I toss several shovels full of compost onto the adjacent pile to cover the kitchen waste and keep down the numbers of flies, gnats, and yellow jackets. After pulling the third cart up the hill to the back of the house, I am ready for work.

I plant basil in the pots at the edge of the brick patio and then dig out *Phalaris arundinacea* var. picta and deceased nut sedge below the kitchen window. With my garden fork I dig deeply into the hard soil and put half a bucket of compost on each of four areas. I dig some more and turn the soil until the color turns from gray-brown to near black. Finally I plant the remaining four basil plants and sprinkle Plant-tone all around them. I dig in the corms of Tigridia among the plants of nigella with ripening seeds. Following that, I water my new plantings and carry one of the carts to the mulch pile where I bring up a heaping load of shredded leaves. These are spread onto the beds.

I carry a cart at a time to the shrub border, stopping along the way to dig out pokeweeds, ampelopsis, and weedy grasses. I plant two pots of the very large castor bean, *Ricinus zanzibariensis,* and all of the gladiolus corms. From there I go to the soft color, again carrying all three carts. By now one of the carts is half full of weeds. I plant a lantana in the large pot at the edge of the soft color garden. It has flowers in shades of pale yellow and pink and will be perfect to blend with the other creamy and pale colored flowers in that bed. I put the new salvia on the other side of the garden. The four other Ricinus are put into the back of the aster border where eventually they will tower over all of the plants between them and the walk. Before I can plant them, I have to remove a large number of *Euphorbia lathyris,* which are about to go to seed.

I dig in all of the hymenocallis into the Black and White Garden and then prepare the soil for planting sunflowers (helianthus) into the Blue and Yellow Garden. I dig in the two remaining buckets full of compost. Finally, I turn on the well and water all of these plants slowly and deeply. I return all of the tools to my cart—the one with the sagging handle— carry the weeds to the brush pile, and pull all three carts back to their places beneath the law office.

By now it is 2:00 PM and, although rain is in the forecast, I don't trust it; so I spend the remainder of the afternoon watering the nursery stock, shady cold frames, Walter's bench, and carry two gallon watering cans filled with water from the containers at the edge of the barn to the *Davidia involucrata* and *Stewartia malacodendron* at the edge of the woods. I pull out the hose from beneath the figs and water the plants in containers near the garage, on the bank, and near the wood-splitter.

The storms do come. Although I don't mind getting wet, I am afraid of lightning. I go inside shortly after 7:00, hot, dirty, tired, and very happy with this quiet solitary day.

NANCY GOODWIN is a renowned gardener and the author of several books, including *Montrose: a Life in the Garden* and *A Year in Our Gardens* (with Allen Lacy). She lives at historic Montrose in Hillsborough with her husband, Craufurd Goodwin, an economics professor at Duke University; Angie, their energetic four-legged adviser; and three cats.

Dog Hunting

JILL McCORKLE

A COUPLE OF YEARS AGO MY HUSBAND, Tom, and I were out walking in the woods. He had his gun in case he saw something he thought he should shoot. I didn't have a gun which is a good thing as I don't know the first thing about them, so I was perfectly happy to walk around, listening to the birds and then the wind while momentarily we rested and perched way up a tree in a deer stand. There wasn't a whole lot happening that day as far as I could tell, except that it was a really nice time to be outside.

After the quiet time, we walked around again only to find one of our neighbors propped against a tree. He was wearing camouflage and blended right in except for the orange cap, which is what startled us into seeing him. We stopped and talked for a little while, as he had no trouble talking. He was very skilled at hunting and telling a story, and glimpsing his verbal talent affirmed to me that this was indeed a good way to spend my afternoon. *I can do this,* I was thinking. *I can hunt words — catch, skin, and string them into nice long colorful sentences.*

It seemed this was all we would find that quiet afternoon but we kept walking off toward the river, still hoping we might see something Tom might want to shoot. I have to confess here that I am someone who has no experience whatsoever with hunting and was surprised that I was even out there at all. But I was and also was relieved that I didn't witness Bambi on the run or Thumper shivering in the bushes. Let's just say I was not pre-pared to haul something dead or dying.

What I did see was a little pack of beagles with wires sticking up out of their collars like they were on remote. They came out of nowhere — wig-gling wind-up toys with wagging tails, snorting and sniffing the ground. There were three brown and whites about the same size — let's call them Larry, Curly, and Moe — who were stumbling and rolling all over each other, and then there was the leader — a black and white beagle who looked just like her name: Dottie. And how did we know her name? Because some man was yelling, "Dottie? Dottie?"

At first I thought the voice was coming from one of the trio and that we had stumbled on The Famous Talking Dog. An *If a dog talks out in the woods and there's no one to hear him . . .* sort of thing. But then we glimpsed a man (also wearing orange) way off in the distance and it was clear that he was a little upset with Dottie. She had stopped doing what she was supposed to be doing. She was a working girl out to survey the territory and the little wire in her collar was her global positioning system.

I had never heard of "Dog Hunting" but this was what I was witnessing. It isn't as bad as it sounds. It's a sport where the dog is co-participant with man, kind of like Frisbee. The object of this sport is for the dogs to sniff out and run deer up and out to where their master men can rise up from where they've been slouched against the trunk of a tree or hiding up in its branches, maybe drinking and talking a little, aim and shoot.

Clearly Dottie was tired and taking a little break. The man kept on bellowing her name but she didn't seem to give a damn what he said or what he wanted. She and Larry, Curly, and Moe were deep in the woods, the Eno River within view and she was far more interested in what the boys were doing which was sniffing us, peeing, and humping one another.

"Dottie. Dottie. Go girl."

Dottie did not give one single damn. I think if a deer had walked right up, Dottie would have looked the other way. She was on strike and who could blame her? It was a scene right out of *Lady Chatterley's Lover*. Dottie and her handsome suitors deep in the woods, the river rushing, the wind blowing. It was idyllic, not a deer in sight. It's a dog sport. It's what they do when they stop listening to people and get together in the middle of the woods.

JILL McCORKLE is the author of nine books, including *July 7th*, *The Cheerleader*, and *Going Away Shoes*. Five of her books have been selected as New York Times Notable Books. She is the recipient of the North Carolina Award for Literature, the John Dos Passos Prize for Excellence in Literature, and many other awards. She teaches writing at North Carolina State University.

Deer Drives

CRAIG NOVA

SOME YEARS AGO, I used to hunt deer with my father-in-law, who owned a piece of land on the Delaware River in New York. Frankly, we had an adversarial relationship, although I think that underneath it all we had a profound respect for one another. While we would see who could drive a car the fastest or who could take the biggest chance, we nevertheless understood one another in a way that I think few people do. That is, when he died, I went to pick up his ashes from the mortuary, and I realized, as I picked up the bag that held the box, we were communicating. I understood then that he knew that I was the only one he could trust for the job. And so, as I was suspended in a state of understanding that was so close to tears as to leave me a little frightened, I thought about how we hunted deer together.

The piece of land my father-in-law owned was about fifteen hundred acres. A section of it swept from the top, about five hundred feet above the Delaware, to the river itself, and in the middle of this sloping landscape was a sort of gulley or wide swale. It was a perfect place for a deer drive, and when my father-in-law invited his friends and former classmates to hunt deer, he liked to organize a deer drive through this swale.

It worked this way. Three or four men stood at the place where the swale opened up at the river. The rest of us spread out at the top of the land in a line, five or six hundred yards long, and then began walking toward the place where the four men were standing. There is an art to this. It should be done slowly, very slowly. A little noise should be made. Some of us tapped two sticks together to make a clicking sound. The idea was that the deer would move a hundred yards or so away from us at a sedate walk, and then stop and look back over their shoulders. Ideally, they would do this when they were right in front of the standers, who, of course, would have all the time in the world to aim for that spot just behind the deer's shoulder.

Actually, I saw this entire process as part of a recipe ("Take a deer of the season . . .") since this was the only way I knew to have one of my favorite dinners: a crown roast of venison with morels. Roast potatoes. Broccoli flowers. A chocolate soufflé for dessert.

In fact, eating was a large part of the activity of hunting deer, and my father-in-law and I ate a bushel of oysters together during one deer hunt.

My wife and I lived on this land and I ran it as a tree farm, which meant I spent a lot of time in the woods, and the things I saw there — foxes, ruffed grouse, bears, deer, snakes — worked their way into the book I was writing. The book had a deer hunt in it, done, oddly enough, in much the same way that we drove the main gate (what we called the drive down the swale to the river). The book also contained a woman naturalist's diary, in which a character wrote about the things she saw. In particular, I remember a day when I was working on the book in the house, and looked out the door as a flock of wild turkeys went by. As they walked along, a gobbler in front, a gobbler at the rear, I wrote them right into the book.

My wife and I eventually left there and moved to Vermont, where we had children and where I stopped hunting deer, although I kept bird dogs for awhile, but finally I let them go, too, sold my deer rifles and shot guns, and pounded my sword into a ploughshare, that is, I bought a King Racing single and starting rowing. I realized I could have children and be a father to them, or I could spend all my time training bird dogs. The dogs went.

However, I have to say that you don't forget the things you've learned, and that once an activity has been encoded, it is right there, waiting to be used. Just think how quickly you respond to a voice on the phone that says, "Hey, this is a voice from your past. . . ."

Recently, I've had the chance to put this theory to the test. Not long ago, my wife and I moved to Hillsborough, and we met Nancy Goodwin, a lovely, inspiring woman who happens to be a great gardener. I can't remember where I first met her, but I know that there was something in her eyes, a certain knowing intelligence that I have seen a couple of times and always with a sort of shock. The first person I saw with this expression was a Maine bush pilot by the name of Jack McPhee. He was at once friendly and precise, and when I stayed in a cabin he had on a pond you had to reach by air, I went outside and looked at the axe he had there for cutting firewood: The edge was sharp, silver colored. Like a piece of Christmas tinsel. Jack McPhee all over.

Nancy Goodwin has a garden, quite a large one, and I think that after some years she grew exasperated with the fact that while the climate for Hillsborough could allow some lovely plants and flowers to grow, the deer in town would eat them down to the ground. So, having the same resolve as a bush pilot in Maine, Nancy decided to do something about it. She built a fence around the twenty or so acres of her garden.

Now, while deer are in many ways exceedingly smart and naturally wary, so much so that they can be surprising, they make mistakes, too. When I was hunting deer on a piece of land where a book of mine is set, deer-hunting season in Pennsylvania, across the river, had not opened yet even though it had in New York. Deer were seen swimming, and swimming fast, I might add, across the Delaware from New York to Pennsylvania on the night before the season opened in New York. So, you would think that the deer in Hillsborough would know that Nancy Goodwin was building a fence, and that if the deer weren't careful, they would be trapped inside.

Perhaps the deer had the innate sense to realize that if they were inside, other deer would be trapped outside, and so the deer inside the fence, like human beings in Eden, would have an advantage over the poor souls outside. That is, the deer inside would have the first whack at the things that deer like.

The fence was built. The deer were trapped inside. And, of course, Nancy Goodwin had the experience that I have had many, many times before when I have often tried to do one thing, only to find that I am really doing something else. This is part of the writer's experience, because often they are misunderstood. For instance, when Upton Sinclair wrote *The Jungle,* he was concerned about how the human beings were being treated in the meatpacking industry. But his readers were only concerned about how the sausage was made.

So, when Nancy Goodwin, who had read a book of mine in which a hunt is described, called to ask if I could help with her deer, so perfectly trapped inside the fence, I found myself putting down the phone and staring out the window. What I remembered were those fall afternoons in New York when we drove the deer toward the main gate, and, in particular, I recalled walking through a dry swamp where a copperhead, sluggish from the cold and not yet denned up, wiggled under my boot: a sensation at once familiar and oddly old. Or the shapes of the flights of geese, V-shaped, like the eel traps in the Delaware River and the constant ache of that honking. Well, I thought, maybe this time we can drive deer, not to kill them, but to save the garden. And it occurred to me that there was something biblical in this: We would act like the archangels, Gabriel for instance, who drove Adam and Even out of Eden.

Hillsborough is a town that pulls together, so when I asked around to see if people would be willing to help, the citizens lined up. The most important thing, or so it seemed to me, was to make sure we had enough drivers to walk across the land, and to do so spaced evenly so that the deer couldn't run between us. The beauty of Nancy Goodwin's fence is that on one side it has three gates: My theory was that we could line up opposite these gates and then walk toward them. They, of course, would be left open. Then the deer would be driven through them, out of Eden.

First, I had to figure out what the distance should be between drivers. Since I wasn't quite sure how many would actually show up on the day of the drive, I made a little chart, a sort of actuarial table, which showed how many feet (or, actually, how many fence posts) should be left between drivers, depending on how many we had. The more people we had, of course, the less distance we would leave between them.

The day arrived. The odd thing was the strangely festive atmosphere about the entire endeavor. For me, the atmosphere of a deer drive was one of getting ready to shoot these animals, and while I had no problem in doing that, given the fact that the carrying capacity of the land in winter was such that many deer were going to starve to death, the deer hunts of the past seemed somehow more serious. Maybe because we were concerned about a possible accident, or someone getting shot.

And then there was another fact of human existence that showed itself here as it had in the hunts long ago. In the midst of trying to do anything, whether it is starting or managing a battle, or driving deer, somehow, in the middle, communications will break down, people will get lost, and you will be uncertain as to what is really going on. The fog of the deer drive was about to begin.

We all lined up and began walking. At first, I thought that we should try to walk slowly, since I wanted to give the deer plenty of time to amble out toward the gate on the other side of the land. But while I thought we should go slow, I also wanted to make sure that the deer knew we were coming. So, I went out and got some noise-makers, the kind of things that kids have at birthday parties. We lined up. We began.

Another theory, which I didn't mention when we began, was to take advantage of a study I had read years before about how deer are able to hide. The study had men walk through a section of swampy land, which deer love, and to do so walking close together. The deer had radio transmitters on them, so the people conducting the study knew right where they were. The men walked through the cover, and some came as close as a few feet to the deer that were hiding in the brush. So, I thought I would walk behind the line of drivers, swinging back and forth, and look into every pile of brush, every bit of cover where a deer could hide.

Of course, we moved too fast, and soon the deer started to run. And since it was hard to keep the line straight, it was hard to know, given what I heard, exactly what was happening. Some of the people had seen the deer running, not in the gentle, canter-like movement they make when they bound through the woods, but in the more streaking, earnest, ground-covering run that deer make when they are really scared. While some of the deer had gone out the gate, or most of them had, I hoped, one deer ran headlong into the fence and broke its neck.

But even then the past seemed to linger: since, as some other members of the drive were horrified, I thought of field dressing the thing, stringing it up, and letting it hang for a little before cutting it into a couple of crown roasts of venison. The only thing that stopped me was the sanguine nature of such an activity and the fact that I still remembered the law: If a deer is killed by mistake out of season, the correct thing to do is to call the police if you were going to use the meat. Otherwise, it was best to let nature take its course, and let the coons and vultures go to work.

We drove the land again to make sure we hadn't missed any deer, and then, like archangels having avenged ourselves on the innocent, we closed the gates.

And then waited. That was the worst time, as it is in any action done for a particular result that isn't immediately obvious. Did we get them all? Were they still there? Nancy and I consulted the next day: Apparently a fawn had been trapped or left inside, and the fawn and mother communicated, or so it seemed, through the fence. And then the fawn disappeared, too.

These two drives so perfectly compressed time that I am still a little disoriented. I can't go by Nancy's fence without thinking of those years, long ago, when we hunted deer and heard that endless honking of the geese, that tugged so profoundly at one's sense of time and mortality. And, of course, another matter lurks around in all of this, which has something to do with what it is like to be human and to take action: The human condition, as it is so becomingly called, can be seen in this. No matter how much the motive in this drive had changed, and no matter how I was only trying to save beauty, it still came at a price, since no matter when, either years ago when I hunted deer in New York, or drove them away to save a garden in Hillsborough, a deer died.

CRAIG NOVA is the author of twelve novels, including *The Good Son* and *Cruisers*. His most recent novel is *The Informer*, published by Shaye Areheart. He is a recipient of an Award in Literature from the American Academy and Institute of Arts and Letters and is currently the Class of 1949 Distinguished Professor in the Humanities at the University of North Carolina, Greensboro.

Going Up the Country

JOHN VALENTINE

WHEN WE FIRST FOUND OUR FOUR-ROOM, wood-stove-heated little house at the end of a rutted, packed clay drive in 1972, the road that led home wasn't paved. A lot of turn-offs from St. Mary's Road in rural Hillsborough were dirt back then. I drove an old, faded maroon Volkswagen van with a roll-top roof, a platform bed, a 6-volt battery, and a dozen windows. Going down hills, I'd floor it just to make it up the other side.

After heavy rains, I'd have to park the van. It couldn't handle those slippery inclines. Once, I didn't park it so well, and it back rolled through a cornfield, just missing a little creek.

That first turn of the seasons in our new house was glorious. A dairy farmer, our road was named after his father, sold us unpasteurized milk. A local commercial chicken farmer gave us manure for our garden. We developed a taste for homegrown okra! We canned many jars of green beans and tomatoes. Someone was always making yogurt, granola or baking bread. Our extended family doubled in size every weekend with visitors. We were always outnumbered by dogs, cats, and chickens.

On new moons, we would gather quilts and sleeping bags and head for an open field to watch for comets and shooting stars. On full moons we were enchanted. That first December we cut down a weedy roadside pine for our Christmas tree.

One blustery spring, a brush fire started down by a creek bed and blew out of control. It swept toward houses and barns. Local firefighters arrived just as the blaze jumped the road. Their tools of choice were snub-nosed Bobcats with sturdy plows. They crisscrossed the forests, building fire-breaks. It worked. Those breaks are now meandering paths lined with ferns.

I often wander those paths and surrounding woods, watching for signs and noticing the changes. Once, two local farmers, one black, one white, from different sides of the road, asked me to walk the shared corners of our property with them. Landowners on our road trust rock piles and their memories more than survey maps. Patiently walking through the woods those afternoons, we found rusty iron pipes and large flat stones that had served as property markers for fifty years. One man counseled, "This is so you and my daughters know what's what."

With all its twists and turns, our road offers plenty of bucolic views and blind spots. Blind spots are little tucks in the road, like oxbow curves, where you are hidden from oncoming traffic. For kids growing up in the suburbs, where neighbors usually see everything, blind spots offer new mysteries and surprises. It's in those blind spots that people dump stuff. All kinds of stuff. An old television set, a washing machine, a truck bed full of roofing tiles, a litter of puppies. You name it, we've seen it, straddling a ditch, sur-rounding a stump, leaning against a culvert. It takes about three minutes, I figure, to pull over to the side and off-load just about anything.

When this was a dirt road, you couldn't drive faster than forty miles an hour and still get from A to B in one piece. Back then, on a good day, when the wind blew right, you could hear the cars racing at the nearby old Orange County Speedway. The speedway closed, and our road, now paved, with its own attractive banked turns seems to have taken its place.

Faster traffic means less time at your preferred blind spot. You've got to be quick while unloading all of your ex's stuff these days.

Not to totally slam dumping. A few days ago, in fact, a local historian was wandering the roads with a GPS system, mapping an old Indian trading path from Roxboro to Hillsborough. It curled right around our row of power lines. After main roads overtook old trading paths, local farmers used those old roadways as dumps. Look around and you'll find piles of discarded Mason jars, a few cobalt blue treasures with wire-top closures, and rusted-out trash burners yielding charred curios of country life a century ago.

Out here, we're holding on to our clunkers. There are four kinds of pickup truck drivers: the speeders, the dumpers, the hunters, and the recyclers. Most of us are members of at least two of those groups. The other day, for instance, somebody backed three truckloads of tree debris into an abandoned driveway. On an overcast Saturday morning, I took possession of that mess—a massive mound of sawdust, limbs, and quartered stumps of white oak. It took longer to load it into my truck than it had taken someone to unload it. I can't wait for the first frost. The wood stove will be humming.

The long gone dairy farm is now coveted real estate, rolling fields bordering the road and a river. The hog farm on the corner magically reinvented itself as a favorite summer destination, a pick-your own-strawberry farm!

Another neighbor runs a barbecue business on the side. He makes coleslaw. About once a month, he leaves a box with a few heads of cabbage in the underbrush on one of the road's curves. For our chickens used to a sensible diet of cracked corn, cabbage is like ice cream. They just have to get to it while it's green. And we have to watch out for the blind spots.

JOHN VALENTINE is a chief contributor to the *Independent Weekly*. He was an original "Our Lives" columnist in the Raleigh *News & Observer*. He is co-owner of the Regulator Bookshop on Ninth Street in Durham.

Stop Your Engines

KATHARINE WHALEN

THE OCCONEECHEE SPEEDWAY'S DAYS as a racing attraction are long gone. Trees now grow thickly in the center of the oval dirt racetrack, where NASCAR drivers once competed. The concrete grandstand and giant wooden poles that held the lights and loud speakers are still there, ghostly reminders of the speedway's past. It's quiet and slightly eerie if you stop to imagine race days with cars roaring by, crowds cheering, and movie stars like Jayne Mansfield making appearances. (She really did visit as Guest of Honor on March 10, 1963. I envision her standing on the track between the cars, brandishing the starting flag to begin the race.)

I always feel almost famous here because of my trumpet player's father's cousin, Dink Widenhouse #B29, who raced a 1940 Ford Standard with the fins cut off on this track in the early 1950s. Cool daddy-o! The list of Occoneechee drivers through the years read like a *Who's Who* of early NASCAR . . . Bill France, Fonty Flock, Junior Johnson, and Richard Petty, they all drove here.

The speedway closed in 1968, after a twenty-year run. According to local lore, NASCAR had wanted to expand its Hillsborough site, but some local religious leaders protested, not wanting the town to be dominated by car racing. The little Alabama town of Talladega stepped forward and NASCAR became part of our local history.

The track is still an important community attraction, but without the cars. These days everyone's on foot. We pay tribute to its former glory by calling it the *Historic* Occoneechee Speedway. It's a peaceful 204-acre park. Forking off the old racetrack is a well-tended system of trails (called traces).

When you begin winding around on these you come to the Eno River, and at one point can peer over into the Ayr Mount estate, site of the Poet's Walk, another great local trail. Lining the river bank on the Occoneechee Speedway trails are stately beech trees, which have been guarding this river for a long time. Lunch under the canopy of one of these leafy grandparents is a peaceful experience.

Here's my Occoneechee Picnic Essentials, A Partial List:

— *Blanket.* The Ultimate to me is a vintage football blanket, made of sturdy plaid wool and a deeply pleasing, perfect square shape.

— *Food.* Your choice, but I implore you to visit the "Fancy" section at your grocers for mustard, pickles, chutneys, and other condiments. If they are truly "fancy" they will come in tiny containers, perfect for picnicking!

— *Corkscrew and an Old-Man's Briarwood Pipe.* Even if you don't drink, you will appear Worldly if you have a corkscrew. Of course, you don't smoke the pipe, but you can clamp it in your teeth grimly, while you make witty remarks to your companions.

—*Newspaper with many sections to spread out for After Lunch Napping.* Perhaps a *New York Times.* It is a proven fact that you can become smarter and more informed through osmosis. Cats know this. Take heed.

—*Assorted Friends and Relations.* If anyone you know and love makes you slightly claustrophobic, a picnic is the perfect way to visit with this individual.

KATHARINE WHALEN is a northern Orange County artist, picnicker, guest columnist for the local paper, and musician. She continues to perform with the popular Squirrel Nut Zippers and her new group, Katharine Whalen's Lucky.

Views From Before

For We Were Once a Wayside Inn

JEFFERY BEAM

The Old Road

After William Bartram

I pass steep rocky ascents

enter a charming vale

My winding path leads me over green fields

into meadows

into labor   industry

simplicity without fallacy or guile

Most perfect hospitality
Most intrepid happy people

Occaneechi

Country town

built round a field

★

Visiting moss landscapes of Orange County
torpid thoughts relieve

One re-lives singular regeneration
The mind's minerals the hands recognitions

Caroline

After John Lawson

As to my memory
wild
        spontaneous flowers

So liberal al-
                most unnamable

The copperhead

reminds the cat
attention supersedes
fortitude

★

Think trees they
think of something in return

Think horses standing sleeping they
stand in the mind a long time

Think turtles racing green shadows
shadows remake themselves yellow ribbons

Think cornfields flattened in rain
coons rabbits dance a lively dance

Think lost pigeons once blackening sky
Blue home blue home blue home

Think Eno-waters
your face mirrors susurrant snake ripples

Think cedars keeping stalwart watch
berries promising blue jay indigo bluebird

Think morning and evening the first day
Fortunate land cardinal's Eden

Green home green home green home

★

For we were once
a wayside inn

Too comfortable for words

JEFFERY BEAM is a poet, singer, editor, and photographer. His books of poetry include *Gospel Earth* (Skysill Press), *The Beautiful Tendons* (White Crane Books), *Visions of Dame Kind* (The Jargon Society), and *An Elizabethan Bestiary: Retold* (illustrated by Ippy Patterson, published by Horse & Buggy Press). He is the creator of the spoken word collection, *What We Have Lost: New and Selected Poems, 1977–2001.*

A Temple of Justice Amidst Temples of the Lord:

A view of courthouse & churches in Hillsborough

BROOKS GRAEBNER

NOTHING BETTER SYMBOLIZES Historic Hillsborough than the façade of the Old Courthouse, with its Doric columns, gracious portico, and handsome cupola housing the Colonial-era town clock. Images of the courthouse, designed and built in 1844–45 by local contractor and brick mason John Berry, grace guidebooks and town histories. And even though the Orange County Courthouse complex now extends to several newer, larger buildings, the Old Courthouse still serves its original purpose and remains a significant site for public events.

So accustomed are we to seeing the Old Courthouse that it requires a deliberate act of historical reconstruction to imagine what Hillsborough would have looked like before it was erected. In the early 1840s, the town had four prominent public buildings: three made of brick; one of frame construction. The three brick buildings were the Presbyterian

Church, built in 1816, and the Masonic Hall and St. Matthew's Episcopal Church, both built in 1825 and designed by State Architect William Nichols. The more modest frame building, built in 1790, was the courthouse. By 1840 the fifty-year-old courthouse would have suffered in comparison to the other public buildings in size, design, and materials. A new, larger brick courthouse would remedy this disparity.

Speaking at the laying of the cornerstone for Hillsborough's new courthouse in September 1844, the Rev. William Mercer Green, former rector of St. Matthew's, traced the impetus for this new endeavor to the according of due respect to the institution of the Court itself. "It is to our Churches, our School-houses, our Colleges, and Courts of Civil & Criminal Law" that we owe our national prosperity, he asserted. And of these bulwarks of national well-being, he continued, two stand uppermost: the influence of law and religion. Thus Green proclaimed:

182

> In the structure this day so auspiciously begun, behold one of the strong citadels of yr. defense.... Next to the Sanctuary of the Most High, then revere its very stones, bow to its authority, uphold its influence, and from its impartial sentence take no appeal but to the still higher tribunals of the Country and to yr. God. In the Officer that fulfils its behests, and executes its judgements [sic] see the impersonated authority of the State. Aid him then fearlessly in the discharge of his duty, for he is clothed with the authority of yr. Country & yr. God.[1]

Green's views are consistent with those of other nineteenth-century Americans who regarded the courthouse, not only as a place of assembly, but also as a "temple of justice." Underscoring this view was the use of ancient Greek and Roman temples as forms to emulate in designing courthouses. Thus, Orange County's new 1844–45 courthouse, executed in the style of the Greek Revival, was a fitting expression of the desire to build a structure that would inspire reverence and respect for the rule of law and the institution of the Court itself.[2]

Green considered law and religion as complementary and mutually reinforcing aspects of one overarching divine rule. And he thought that reverence for the majesty and authority of the Court should be second only to the majesty accorded houses of worship. In such a worldview, it would make sense that a courthouse be accorded dignity and grandeur comparable to a church.

In this regard, the cupola atop the 1844–45 courthouse was an especially interesting feature, hearkening back to the first St. Matthew's church of 1768, with its prominent clock tower. The building, designed by John Hawks of Tryon Palace fame, was constructed to impress upon the backcountry of Colonial North Carolina the twin authority of the Royal Government and the Established Church. The town clock, a gift of the Crown, was first installed in the St. Matthew's clock tower and might well have remained there had not the tower been so badly damaged in the Revolutionary War that it had to be demolished. Soon thereafter the church building itself suffered the same fate.

The handsome courthouse designed by John Berry might well be regarded a fitting successor to the first St. Matthew's building, and indeed it has become the lasting home to our well-known town clock. But in the actual setting of 1840s Hillsborough, the cupola-adorned courthouse now had a prominence and a profile unmatched by any of the church buildings still standing. It set a new standard for public buildings. No longer was it enough to have well-proportioned and well-crafted buildings for assembly; in this new post–1845 environment, churches, no less than courthouses, needed spires designed to lift eyes upward and recall the larger symbolic purposes these buildings expressed.

---

1 William Mercer Green, *Address Delivered at the Laying of the Corner-Stone of a New Court-House, at Hillsborough, N. Ca. Sept. 7, 1844.* Typescript in the Papers of Mary Claire Engstrom, Southern Historical Collection, University of North Carolina, Chapel Hill, p. 9. At the time of the address, Green was a professor at the University of North Carolina, Chapel Hill, but he was no stranger to Hillsborough. From 1825 to 1838 he was rector of St. Matthew's Episcopal Church.

2 "Functional, Historical, Architectural and Symbolic Value of the North Carolina Courthouse," in Robert P. Burns, Project Director, *100 Courthouses: A Report on North Carolina Judicial Facilities.* Raleigh: North Carolina State University, 1978, v. I, p. 28.

The first church building to reflect this new aesthetic was Hillsborough Methodist Church. In 1859, the Methodists engaged the services of the very man responsible for the design and construction of the courthouse: John Berry. Not surprisingly, Berry incorporated many of the courthouse design details to his new project. And he gave the church a prominent tower. Later that same year, the Baptists turned to architect William Percival for their design, ultimately relying on the same John Berry to complete the work. Again, the new church building had a tower, and a façade far more imposing than either the Presbyterian or Episcopal churches of an earlier era. The Episcopalians and Presbyterians eventually followed suit, however, adding sizable steeples to their buildings as part of extensive late-nineteenth-century renovation projects.

By 1950, even Hillsborough's former courthouse, built in 1790, had undergone a similar transformation: The congregation of Dickerson Chapel A.M.E. converted the old frame building to a house of worship, clad it in brick, and added an attractive steeple.[3]

The result of all this construction and modification is a set of nineteenth-century public buildings remarkable for their durability, design, and similarity of appearance. That they bear such close family resemblance is no accident. It reflects the vision articulated by William Mercer Green in 1844, a vision that guided the construction of Hillsborough's courthouse and churches for much of its history: the desire to foster an ordered and pious society of citizen-churchgoers.

---

3 See Brooks Graebner, "The Antebellum Churches of Hillsborough," *Hillsborough Historical Society Journal*, v.7, no.1 (Winter 2004), pp.35–48.

THE REV. BROOKS GRAEBNER has served as rector of St. Matthew's Episcopal Church in Hillsborough since 1990. He is a past president of the Hillsborough Historical Society, and is the Secretary of the Historical Society of the Episcopal Church and the Historiographer of the Episcopal Diocese of North Carolina. He has taught at the University of North Carolina, Chapel Hill, Wake Forest University, and the Duke Divinity School.

who will be the messenger of this land

JAKI SHELTON GREEN

who will be the messenger of this land
count its veins
speak through the veins
translate the language of water
navigate the heels of lineage
who will carry this land in parcels
paper, linen, burlap
who will weep when it bleeds
and hardens
forgets to birth itself

who will be the messenger of this land
wrapping its stories carefully
in patois of creole, irish,
gullah, twe, tuscarora
stripping its trees for tea
and pleasure
who will help this land to
remember its birthdays, baptisms
weddings, funerals, its rituals
denials, disappointments,
and sacrifices

who will be the messengers
of this land
harvesting its truths
bearing unleavened bread
burying mutilated crops beneath
its breasts

who will remember
to unbury the unborn seeds
that arrived
in captivity
shackled, folded,
bent, layered in its
bowels

we are their messengers
with singing hoes
and dancing plows
with fingers that snap
beans, arms that
raise corn, feet that
cover the dew falling from
okra, beans, tomatoes

we are these messengers
whose ears alone choose
which spices
whose eyes alone name
basil, nutmeg, fennel, ginger,
cardamom, sassafras
whose tongues alone carry
hemlock, bloodroot, valerian,
damiana, st. john's wort
these roots that contain
its pleasures its languages its secrets

we are the messengers
new messengers
arriving as mutations of ourselves
we are these messengers
blue breath
red hands
singing a tree into dance

JAKI SHELTON GREEN, the first Piedmont Laureate, has published numerous collections of poetry, including *Dead on Arrival, Conjure Blues, singing a tree into dance,* and *breath of the song* (all published by Carolina Wren Press). Her work has appeared in such publications as *Ms., Essence,* and the *Crucible.* She is the recipient of the North Carolina Award for Literature (2003) and the Sam Ragan Award (2007).

The Journey to Hillsborough

BARRY JACOBS

THE JOURNEY FROM THE NORTH CAROLINA coast to the cooler Occoneechee upcountry took Alfred Moore and family a week by wagon in the late eighteenth century. They came to Hillsborough to stay from May until the first hard frost in October, drawn by the Piedmont town's legal community and the absence of the heat, mosquitoes, disease, and hurricanes of the river country south of Wilmington.

The mosquitoes alone merited avoidance. A 1734 account of life on the lower Cape Fear River said the insects "made nothing to fetch blood of us through our buckskin gloves, coats, and jackets." Considering that another coastal tale, doubtless apocryphal, described a colonial hunter escaping harm when a rattlesnake bit into his buckskin leggings and held fast, these were not mosquitoes to be suffered lightly.

Wealthy and numerous, Moores were prominent in public affairs in the Carolinas for 200 years, starting in 1700 when James Moore became South Carolina's first governor. The governor's son, Maurice Moore, helped found the port of Brunswick, now a state historic site, in 1726 in North

Carolina's Cape Fear region. Members of the clan owned 83,000 acres north of Brunswick, including Alfred Moore's rice plantation, Buchoi (sometimes rendered Beauchoix), and family outposts, such as The Vats, Moore Fields, Kendal, and Orton Plantation, the only surviving Moore manse along the river.

History casts the Moores—considered to be heroes and leaders by the standards of their times—in a harsh light. During the run-up to the American Revolution, family members led military efforts to subdue and eradicate the Tuscarora, Waccamaw, Cape Fear, and other Indians in the Carolina lowlands, clearing the way for development. Moores were among early North Carolina's largest owners of slaves. They defended British authority in the courtroom and on the battlefield.

Maurice Moore (Jr.), Alfred's father, was removed as a colonial judge for writing a pamphlet highly critical of the Stamp Act—imposed by the Crown to offset the cost of maintaining an army in the Colonies—only to be reinstated in time to join judicial colleagues in sentencing six Regulators to be hanged at Hillsborough in June 1771.

A Moore descendent, Captain James Iredell Waddell, commanded the last active Confederate cruiser in the Civil War. The *C.S.S. Shenandoah* continued to sink vessels from the New England whaling fleet off the Alaska coast long after the South's major armies had been disbanded. He then thwarted capture by steaming 17,000 miles to England to surrender to the queen in November 1865.

The captain's first cousin, Colonel Alfred Moore Waddell, was the most prominent white-supremacist leader of the 1898 Wilmington race riot that terrorized the black populace, overthrew the city's integrated leadership, and led to the murder of an untold number of African Americans. Installed as mayor of Wilmington after the legitimate government was ousted, A.M. Waddell had served as an officer in the Confederate cavalry, as an attorney, editor of the *Wilmington Herald* and *Charlotte Observer*, and as a longtime elected official. A much-sought orator, he wrote three books, including *Some Memories of My Life,* an autobiographical reminiscence of boyhood in Hillsborough.

Thanks to Alfred Moore, their great-grandfather, both Waddells had ties to Hillsborough. Moore became acquainted with the town, a center of legal activity and a candidate to become the permanent state capital, as a well-respected private lawyer and, following the Revolution, as North Carolina's third attorney general.

Moore's immediate family had suffered heavy losses early in the war for independence—his father and his father's brother, Continental Army General James Moore, died of disease; his brother Maurice (III) was killed in action, as was his brother-in-law, Francis Nash. In 1781 the British plundered Alfred Moore's Cape Fear home after he refused to cease guerilla activities as a colonel in the American militia near Wilmington. "Tell your commander that I cannot be corrupted into indifference for my country," Moore declared, "that I will struggle in her defense as long as I can get five men to march with me."

Moore's appointment as attorney general was in part recompense for his personal losses. He apparently made a quick financial recovery, amassing 1,202 acres some three miles southwest of the courthouse in Hillsborough. There, surrounded by fifty oaks planted for shade, atop one of the higher spots in Orange County, family legend has it Alfred Moore assigned seven men, presumably from among his numerous slaves, to build a summer residence. Construction of the two-story house at Moorefields began around the time Moore became attorney general and was completed three years later in 1785. By then, Moore County had been established and named in his honor.

Fourteen years later, having served as a state legislator, a founder of the University of North Carolina, and a superior court judge, Alfred Moore was appointed to the U.S. Supreme Court by President John Adams. The second and last North Carolinian to reach the high court, he served under Chief Justice John Marshall and retired due to ill health in 1804. Justice Moore died in 1810.

Moorefields passed to Alfred Moore's namesake son, at one time speaker of the North Carolina House, and remained in family hands into the twentieth century. It was there, in the 1830s, that thirteen-year-old James Iredell Waddell moved from Pittsboro to live with his grandparents and finish his education at Hillsborough's Bingham School. In 1841 he joined the U.S. Navy, sailing off more than two decades later to blubber-busting fame as a Confederate raider in Aleutian waters.

"It is singular that the deviltry which my playmates' mothers invariably ascribed to me went on as of old, and that I lost all desire for that amusement after leaving Chatham County," wrote the taciturn Captain Waddell. "Perhaps the breezes of a loftier region sweeping over the red hills of old Orange purified my heart." Then again, based on his Confederate service, including a contemplated bombardment of San Francisco in August 1865, perhaps not.

Younger cousin Alfred Moore Waddell was born in 1834 at Moorefields, his great-grandfather's retreat south of the Eno River near Seven Mile Creek. The property "lies in the midst of an undulating country, abundantly watered by small rocky streams and heavily wooded by every kind of forest tree indigenous to the middle belt of the Atlantic States," Waddell wrote in 1907 in *Some Memories of My Life*. He recalled a spring-fed stream cooling a rock-built dairy, and all manner of flowers and trees cultivated around the small Federal-style house. He also reported "a greater variety of good fish in the streams and more small game in the fields and woods than, perhaps, anywhere else in the State."

Growing up at Moorefields, educated at Bingham School and Caldwell Institute, Alfred Moore Waddell knew a Hillsborough strikingly different than it is today:

> No railroad with its roaring train and shrieking whistle had then waked
> the echoes of the Occoneechee hills which overlooked the village. The
> old-fashioned four-horse stage, whose advent was announced a half
> mile away by the strident notes of a long tin horn — the pride of the

heavily bearded driver, the crack of whose whip above his leaders was like a pistol-shot — was the traveler's means of conveyance, and the bearer of the mails; and its arrival was greeted by an assemblage of citizens who didn't expect anything particular in the way of correspondence, but hankered after the news. . . . While the Mexican war was in progress [1846–48] the arrival of the stage was the most exciting event in the life of the town, because a number of soldiers had gone from Orange and the adjoining counties, and great anxiety was felt as to their fate.

Waddell's book boasted of the esteemed membership of the Orange County Bar, which during a discrete span included chief justices, and members of the state supreme court, secretaries of the navy, and members of Congress, the state legislature, and the state courts. His interest was more than professional; during Waddell's youth, legal proceedings also provided the occasional authorized escape from classes.

Whenever a case of importance was to be tried the boys at school were given a holiday in order that they might hear the great lawyers speak, and they never failed to take advantage of the privilege. I remember several such cases and the effects they produced upon the boys who heard the trials. One or two that I recall were murder cases, in which the prisoners were convicted and hanged, and of course the boys witnessed the executions, for there is no horror great enough to suppress the eager curiosity of a school boy.

After leaving Hillsborough, Waddell was deeply involved in national politics. At the outbreak of the Civil War in 1861, he took a train from his home in Wilmington to Charleston to witness the bombardment of Fort Sumter. He served four terms in the U.S. Congress, was an alternate delegate (for John Bell) to the Constitutional Union convention in 1860, a Democratic delegate for presidential candidates Winfield Hancock in

1880 and William Jennings Bryan in 1896, and an at-large elector for Grover Cleveland in 1888.

Perhaps his interest in affairs of state was kindled by passions vividly recalled from his youth, when he said "politics ran high" in Hillsborough and animosity was rife between Whigs and Democrats:

> No election day ever passed without numerous fisticuffs, and some-
> times there were very serious "free fights" in which large numbers were
> engaged and blood was freely spilled. I remember one such occasion
> when the entire court-house square seemed to be a struggling mass of
> fighting men. These occasions, it is hardly necessary to say, were red
> letter days for the school boys, who missed no part of the performance,
> and experienced unmitigated delight in following up the combatants.

The Whig party is long gone, as is Hillsborough's courthouse square and the notion the town is a mountainous, backcountry haven. What does endure is spirited political combat (happily of the verbal variety), the house and much-reduced acreage at Moorefields, and the sense that reaching Hillsborough is well worth the journey.

BARRY JACOBS is a journalist and historian, and has written for numerous national, regional, and local publications. He is the author of five books, most recently *Across the Line,* a history of pioneering black basketball players in the South. He is executive director of the Moorefields Foundation, dedicated to preserving the National Register house and grounds at Moorefields.

The Name Game

TOM MAGNUSON

BEFORE HILLSBOROUGH was *Hillsborough*, it was *Childesburg*, and before that, *Corbinton*, and before that, *Orange*. Predating Orange, the oxbow of the Eno that would one day be named and renamed was the site of a native settlement called *Acconeechi*. What the place was called before the mapmakers arrived or the first trader unburdened his packhorse and laid out his goods in Indian Field is anyone's guess.

Unraveling history often involves guesswork. Clues as to why Hillsborough was known by different names at different times can be traced to the naming conventions through the years. As a rule, the older a place name, the more meaning one can divine. Native and early European names tended to describe a recognizable feature—a waterfall, bluff, or peculiar ridgeline (Grandfather Mountain, for example). In the Contact Era, before market farming, when the frontier was largely a subsistence culture, place names were informative, telling travelers of promise or threat or landmarks. Early names, one can say, had survival value.

At least seventy North Carolina names from then started with *Wolf*; about a hundred included the word *Buck*. Other names began with *Bear, Turkey, Buffalo,* and *Rattlesnake* (which may have deterred more settlers than it attracted). *Sassafras* was and continues to be popular, currently part of the name of twenty-eight places in the state.

European mapmakers named Native American villages for an area's dominant people. As mentioned above, the earliest map to unambiguously note the place that would become Hillsborough, the Moseley Map (1733), marks this area as *Acconeechi*[1] with a stamp of two wigwams, one at the great bend in the Eno and the other a couple miles downstream at Indian Field. Acconeechi most likely was a trade town and a safe place for traders to spend a night, thus mapmakers knew its location and name.

Eventually, Europeans who settled here also had their names attached to the place — e.g., *Corbinton* — following the European tradition of naming a place for a dominant individual rather than its people. Near Acconeechi was a settlement called *Eno Will's Town* (and also known as *Adshusheer*). Eno Will was a Coree (a tribe that spoke an Algonquian language) married to an Occaneechi (who spoke a Siouan language). The Siouan were matrilineal, with social status flowing through the female line. Not realizing that Eno Will was merely the husband of an important woman, the English presumed the village was his and assigned it his name. Unfamiliar social norms and numerous tongues side by side threw the European interlopers for a loop. On the backcountry frontier, multiple languages ensured places had multiple names.

Since the earliest chronicles of the area's development, the chief landmarks have been the *monadnock* called Occoneechee Mountain and the Great Bend in the Eno River, where the stream bed slams into the mountain

196

1 Occaneechi, Akenatzy, Akanazy, Acconeechy, Aconeechy, A[c]conichy are all variations on the same name representing the same people. In modern times these folk call themselves Occaneechi, and, when not referring to a specific early usage, that is the spelling used herein. The exception is Occoneechee Mountain.

and makes an abrupt, ninety-degree turn. The Great Bend's dramatic configuration, unique in the central Piedmont, was an almost foolproof inland navigation point.

An eighteenth-century trader leaving Petersburg might have followed these instructions:

> After crossing Moniseep ford on the Roanoke, by midday you will be
> on the Roanoke watershed. Head west on the watershed, and at the end
> of the first day you begin crossing creeks running south. During the
> second day all the streams you cross flow southeast or south. When the
> watershed turns toward the north, veer half left off the watershed and
> head for the forks of the Tar River. Before the end of the day you cross
> the headwaters of the Tar River.
>
> The third day you reach the east branch of the Neuse River, the Flat
> River. Spend the night in the Occaneechi town above the Flat atop Red
> Mountain where the Indians quarry tools from the stone. In the morn-
> ing continue southwesterly. Cross the Flat River just above the forks
> of the river and you will find yourself on a great ridge trail. By midday
> you cross the north fork of the Little River, a major tributary of the Eno.
> Shortly after that you cross the south fork. Then look for left forks off
> the main trail to find a way to the village at the ox bow on the Eno.
> By day's end you will come to the Eno.
>
> If the river flows west to east where you intersect it and high hills
> or bluffs rise on the far side, you are downstream from the Great Bend.
> If the river flows south and no high hills appear on the west side of
> the river, you are upstream from the Great Bend. Make your way to
> the fords near the Great Bend, spend the night with the *Acconeechi*.
> The next morning set your course west of southwest for the fords on
> the Sissipahaw [Haw] River, the middle fork of the Cape Fear River,
> a short day west of the Great Bend on the Eno.

197

Hillsborough may owe much of its eighteenth-century political prominence to the Great Bend. For most of that century until the Revolution, North Carolina's Colonial government was based in New Bern, at the mouth of the Neuse River (the original home of Eno Will's Coree Indians). In early Colonial times the Neuse was called the Eno River all the way from its westernmost headwaters to the coast. Navigating inland was made easy by following the watershed between the Cape Fear River basin and the Neuse basin, the precise route of North Carolina's premier Colonial road, the Great Central Coast Road. (Later it would become Highway 10, and later still Highway 70. Today much of Interstate 40 follows that same ridgeline.) Hillsborough's location at the westernmost point of the Neuse River's main channel was strategic to the government which sought control of its western lands.

Native peoples' names disappear from Colonial records after the Tuscarora War (circa 1715). There is, though, ample evidence that many of them remained here and acquired English names. As with the people so too with the land: *Acconeechi* and the villages near the Great Bend of the Eno were named and renamed according to the whims of the area's new European inhabitants; as they say, name it and it is yours.

Colonial government, long screened from the "backcounty" by the Tuscarora, increasingly asserted itself after the destruction of that people but remained remote even after the 1746 creation of Granville County, Orange County's parent. But with the founding of Orange County (1752), the area was no longer frontier. It was part of a market economy and a new culture based on money and law.

The survival value in place-naming became irrelevant, and appealing to political egos became the new trend. Thus *Acconeechi* faded, and *Orange* was born, perhaps as a ploy by the market-economy elites to curry royal favor by naming the new county seat for William of Orange. When *Orange* no longer seemed important, the town was renamed *Corbinton,* honoring the surveyor who planned and sought a charter for the town. When Corbin fell out of favor, the town was briefly known as *Childesburg* for its Colonial Attorney General.

In 1766, *Childesburg* disappeared from the record, and *Hillsborough* was born. No record details this renaming, but it coincided with the delivery of a tower clock. Possibly Wills Hill, the Earl of Hillsborough, bought naming rights to the town when he presented it with the timepiece that would become its most famous symbol. President of the Board of Trade and Plantations and Secretary of State for the Colonies, the earl is remembered primarily as the man who presided over the disintegration of the crown's North American Colonial holdings. Regardless, Hillsborough gained a town clock (that continues to work) and a name that has endured, with a few bumps along the way.

In the late eighteenth and early nineteenth centuries, Americans rejected most things English. Among the many ways the new nation sought to distinguish itself was by developing an American language, suitable for common folk and stripped of what were deemed unnecessary letters and syllables. Hillsborough dropped its anglicized *ugh* and became *Hillsboro* (as did Pittsborough/*Pittsboro* in Chatham County).

Our much-named town name story almost ends there. But time heals wounds, and tourism promises prosperity. What we once fought, we now embrace. In the mid-sixties, wanting to reclaim its roots with a famed English lord, no matter his ruinous history, *Hillsboro* had its name changed by an official act of the state legislature to *Hillsborough.*

And so it is today, a Colonial name for a town of Revolutionary fame with streets bearing the names of Colonial tyrants of various stripe. History is larded with such ironies.

TOM MAGNUSON is founder and executive director of Trading Path Association and a local historian and . . . man about town, bon vivant, and all round good fellow.

Hillsborough Speaks
(Prologue)

MAX PRESTON

Although I am wrapped in many layers of great and historic events,
today, I, Hillsborough, speak to you of prehistoric things;
I learned this from the land and water themselves.

This mass of land where I stand is looked back upon
as part of Laurentia, a continent which sat in the Iapetus Ocean;
Laurentia gazed across this ocean at a sister land mass called
Gondwana, now Africa and part of South America.

 Forces beneath the earth began to move 570 million years ago.
Gondwana and Laurentia were on a slow collision course
and 270 million years later, the leading edge of Gondwana
crashed into Laurentia with such force, that the place known
as Occoneechee Mountain was thrust upward, attaching itself
to my land. The metamorphosed rock and quartzite,
along with fossilized trilobites, is called "exotic" terrane,
the highest point between the coast and myself.
On this uplift beside me are cliffs and caves, once providing
homes for panthers, bear, and storied mammals,
present today only through brief writings and fossilized bones.
They say I am "exotic"; I am a place of high trails,
flowing streams, ancient flora and fauna—mountain and piedmont.

MAX PRESTON is poet, puppeteer, lawyer, business executive. "Thus," he says, "my nose stays red from sticking it into too many things. I am grateful for all kindnesses and I try to distribute some myself." His earlier collection of poetry is entitled *The Phoenix Collection and Other Poems*.

The Ice House at Burnside

HOLLY REID

IN 2001 ARCHAEOLOGISTS excavated a stone-lined pit at Sixth and Market streets in Philadelphia that once had been part of the Executive Mansion belonging to President George Washington. The dig revealed some unusual discoveries about that pit: It had been Washington's ice house; it was in great condition; and it was in the shape of an octagon.

Hillsborough has its own octagonal ice pit on the old Burnside estate of Paul and Anne Cameron. Meticulously restored by the Preservation Fund of Hillsborough in 2001–02, the ice house today is open to school children, residents, and visitors who can tour this nineteenth-century structure and consider the innovation and work, particularly in the South, once required to make and preserve ice.

Ice forever changed food preservation for cultures used to salting, drying, and smoking their foods. And we have been smitten ever since. This love story influences our lives today in the forms of omnipresent refrigeration and air conditioning, as well as ice so readily available it falls into cups from our refrigerators.

What we now take for granted was in centuries past both revolution-ary and demanding. George Washington gave the frozen commodity great praise in January 14, 1794, when he wrote home to say,

> Do not by any means omit to fill the Ice house with Ice, as the advantages of it for keeping fresh meats &ca, is indescribable.

People of southern climes — like the Washingtons when they returned to Mount Vernon after Philadelphia — were that much more amazed with ice and driven to acquire its immense conveniences. But where did South-erners acquire ice? Where did the Camerons of Hillsborough get the ice to fill the very large ice house at Burnside?

Paul Carrington Cameron and Anne Ruffin were married on Decem-ber 20, 1832, and in 1834 constructed their home, Burnside, on two acres acquired from Anne's father, Thomas Ruffin, on the east side of Hillsbor-ough. The name "Burnside," meaning by the brook or river, was fitting for their home that overlooked the Eno River. However, Paul's preference for planting and dislike of the law profession took the Camerons away from the Orange County seat and back to Fairntosh, his family plantation, northeast of present-day Durham, where they lived for the next twenty-three years.

A need for proper educational opportunities for their children, doctors for a family and enslaved laborers plagued with ill health, and a desire for community were some of the important reasons that drew the Camerons back to Burnside in the mid-1850s. Paul and Anne's love of horticulture and landscaping dominated much of their vision for Burnside. They built many outbuildings, gardens, and an arboretum. It is likely that this was also when the impressive 24-foot-wide, brick-lined, octagonal ice house was constructed.

Anne Ruffin Cameron owned a book entitled *Rural Essays* (Leavitt & Allen, 1853), by A.J. Downing, a famous nineteenth century American horticulturist and landscape designer. The book featured the essay, "How to Build Ice Houses." It is unknown whether the Camerons used this book as a resource in constructing their ice house. Regardless, primary concerns for an ice house success, as Downing noted, were shade, ventilation, and drainage.

The Cameron ice house was located away from the main house in a grove of trees by Spirit Branch, a creek near the eastern boundary of the Cameron estate next to their neighbors, the Grahams. The ice house likely had a steeply pitched roof and perhaps lattice windows under the roof to release warm air. It had a brick drain that led to the nearby creek to ensure that any meltwater would not cover the stored ice, certain doom for its solid state and a common problem for many ice houses.

Even taking these design precautions, most ice-house owners expected to lose at least half the ice they stored. In his 1803 "An Essay on the Most Eligible Construction of Ice Houses and a Description of a Newly-Invented Machine Called the Refrigerator," Thomas Moore wrote, "We must expect a great deal more will be melted than taken out for use." Many wagonloads or sleds of ice, perhaps twenty or thirty tons, would have been required to fill the large Cameron ice house, and likely more than half would trickle down Spirit Branch to the Eno River the ensuing summer.

Records have not yet been found to indicate the Camerons' use of the ice stored in the ice house. It is presumed that it was primarily employed for food preservation and preparation. A receipt was found for a silver ice cream knife, purchased by Paul Cameron's sister, Margaret Mordecai, on January 4, 1859. However, it is important to note that ice was becoming more of a necessity in many households by the mid-1800s. A.J. Downing noted...

Abroad, both the ice-house and the hot-house are portions of the wealthy man's establishment solely. But in this country, the ice-house forms part of the comfort of every substantial farmer. It is not for the sake of ice-creams and cooling liquors, that it has its great value in his eyes, but as a means of preserving and keeping in the finest condition, during the summer, his meat, his butter, his delicate fruit, and, in short, his whole perishable stock of provisions.

At Bodie Plantation in Franklinton, enslaved servant Mary Anderson recalled, "There was a still on the plantation and barrels of brandy were stored in the icehouse, also pickles, preserves and cider." Ice use became the great interest of the dairy, fish, meat, and produce markets. According to Thomas Moore, farmers found they could "entirely supercede the necessity of the unhealthy and disagreeable practice of traveling to market in the night" by using ice and refrigerated containers.

But where did the ice come from for the Cameron family? The probable sources would be from the North (such as the Boston area), from elsewhere in the Piedmont, or from right here in Hillsborough.

Ice From the North

The term *natural ice* refers to ice that has been frozen by weather. Ice production through use of machinery and refrigeration in ice plants or factories didn't become viable until the early twentieth century. The Cameron ice house of the mid-1800s would have stored natural ice.

There are some clues about the sources of natural ice. Paul Cameron wrote a letter to his father-in-law, Thomas Ruffin, in September 1857 when the Camerons took a family trip to New England in hopes of improving the health of one of their daughters. In his letter, Paul remarked about the costly architecture on Frederick Tudor's estate, Nahant, in Massachusetts. This visit could have included a tour of Frederick

Tudor's ice house. But more interestingly, Tudor himself was the renowned "Ice King" of Boston who proved to the unbelieving world that ice transportation was possible over great distances. Tudor shipped ice hand-sawn from fresh ponds (often a perilous activity for horse and human) near Boston to the Caribbean in 1806, and later as far as Calcutta.

Henry David Thoreau witnessed ice-cutters descend on his own Walden Pond:

> Thus it appears that the sweltering inhabitants of Charleston and
> New Orleans, of Madras and Bombay and Calcutta, drink at my
> well. . . . The pure Walden water is mingled with the sacred water
> of the Ganges.

Perhaps the visit to Tudor's estate established a business relationship to ship ice to Hillsborough. About that time, Tudor led Boston shippers in supplying ice to the Southern United States. On the Atlantic seaboard ice was ideal return ballast for ships sailing northward with Southern produce. John Michael Vlach in his book, *The Back of the Big House: The Architecture of Plantation Slavery*, writes:

> In the warmer areas of the Deep South, particularly South Carolina
> and Georgia and the Gulf Coast, a large-scale interstate ice trade
> developed. Beginning in 1799, shiploads of ice were brought in regularly
> from New England . . . consequently ice houses were found all across
> the South.

In addition, Paul Cameron, a champion of increased commerce to the Piedmont and eventually the president of the North Carolina Railroad (1861–62), influenced the location of the railroad through Hillsborough in 1854. The Camerons could afford to import ice by railroad or otherwise. However, if they were involved in the Atlantic ice trade, the Civil War would have completely disrupted it.

Ice From This Region

Where else could the Camerons have procured ice, especially during the Civil War? Richard Kimmel, field archeologist for the U.S. Army Corps of Engineers, has investigated climate records from the 1800s. He found that the nineteenth century was characterized by colder winters and that the difference was significant. For example, Kimmel looked at the diaries of William Wallace White of Vance County, North Carolina, and summarized many years of records between 1857 to 1910:

> Five winters are noted as mild, nine have ice mentioned, 24 years have notes about the ice house being filled, and seven years are considered to be particularly severe.

White's records are consistent with official statistics for that same period. For example, he wrote:

> 1890 = very warm, threatens domestic ice industry; 1893 = very cold, rivers as far south as Wilmington frozen bank to bank.

In parts of the South where ponds and streams froze over during the winter, procuring ice was relatively easy. Clearly, the cooler winter climate of nineteenth century North Carolina allowed the harvesting of natural ice.

Local Ice

Evidence that Vance County, only forty-five miles northeast of Hills-borough, was cold enough to make ice naturally and regularly during the latter half of the nineteenth century begs the question of whether ice could also be produced locally. Personal observation of the Eno River in winter over the past two decades gives the author no confidence of the possibility of natural ice harvest on this running Piedmont river. However, one need only read the first-hand account of Ann Strudwick Nash in her book, *Ladies in the Making*, to find an answer to ice harvesting in Hillsborough.

Miss Nash recounts her days at the Nash-Kollock School on Margaret Lane (now the site of the public library) where some of the Cameron children attended school:

> In the corner nearest the front porch was the well which, if one neglects
> to mention the rain barrels, was the sole source of our water supply.
> The water was cold and crystal clear, and no one ever thought of spoil-
> ing its freshness with ice. In fact ice was still a rare commodity, cut from
> the river if the winter happened to be cold enough, and stored in the
> few ice houses the town afforded. It was muddy and full of bubbles, and
> useful in my eyes chiefly for chilling watermelons and making ice cream.

In another passage Nash regrets not being able to provide ice for an ailing family friend: "I wish it were in our power to contribute to your mother's comfort by sending the ice for which she so much longs, but there was not a pound put up in this place last winter, as we had no season for it."

Finally, Mary Claire Engstrom, local Hillsborough historian, wrote:

> . . . the bitterly cold winter of 1860 was upon them. This was a
> landmark Piedmont winter, savage in its severity, freezing the Eno
> solid and killing scores of pigs, calves and lambs.

These accounts verify the freezing of the Eno River. But two other local sources of ice were probably more reliable than a flowing river. Farmers regularly dug creek- or spring-fed ice ponds on their lands. These ice ponds were quite shallow and are difficult to recognize as historical remnants today. The Camerons had very extensive land holdings, nearly sixty square miles at one point. One or several shallow ice ponds could have been located on Burnside's seventy-five acres, or anywhere else on their holdings. The Camerons also likely traded labor and supplies, and possibly ice, with other successful farms and plantations in the area. Unfortunately, grading for the construction of Cameron Park Elementary School on a portion of the original Burnside grounds in the late 1950s may have eliminated evidence of the possible existence of a shallow ice pond near the ice house.

The other most likely source of ice for the Camerons was the damming of Spirit Branch downhill from the ice house. Brick structural artifacts, which can be seen today perpendicular to the stream, perhaps were abutments for a dam. With enough stream flow and proper catchment, this possible ice pond would have been convenient for harvesting and supplying the ice house located less than a hundred feet away, albeit up a steep incline. A hand-drawn map found in the Cameron Papers shows the orientation of the ice house with the large kitchen garden, stables, orchards, cornfields, and paths. The map's draftsman included a notation of the spring that could have irrigated the Cameron kitchen garden by summer and packed their ice house by winter.

The continued interpretation of the Cameron ice house, as well as many farm and town ice houses in Piedmont North Carolina, is an interesting and important story. Natural ice and its subsequent manifestations in manufactured ice and refrigeration have had a remarkable influence on the American way of life, past and present.

HOLLY REID advocates for environmental and cultural diversity. She has worked as an environmental scientist on air pollution issues in Nepal and the United States. More recently she served as president of the Eno River Association and is co-founder of the Walkable Hillsborough Coalition. She and her family live in an old home on the Eno River in Hillsborough.

[The author would like to acknowledge the following valuable sources of information and inspiration: Bill Crowther and the Preservation Fund of Hillsborough, Jean Anderson, Mary Claire Engstrom, Leah Burt, Barbara Church, Richard Cummings, John Clauser, A J. Downing, John Michael Vlach, Michael Olmert, Henry David Thoreau, Richard Kimmel, Ann Strudwick Nash, UNC's Southern Historical Collection, and Bob Ireland and *Hillsborough Historical Society Journal* for reprint permission from V. 5, No. 1, Fall 2002.]

About the Cover

The cover illustration for 27 *Views of Hillsborough* is the work of Daniel Wallace. A writer and illustrator who lives in Chapel Hill (but visits Hillsborough often), Daniel is a professor at University of North Carolina, Chapel Hill, and frequently the chief judge of the Burwell School's best-dressed dog contest.

His novels include *Big Fish: A Novel of Mythic Proportions* (which was adapted into a major motion picture) and *Mr. Sebastian and the Negro Magician*. His illustrations have appeared in the *Los Angeles Times*, *Italian Vanity Fair*, and many other places.